"The book provides readers with the background in church social teaching they need to understand what the pope is saying. And, best of all, Tornielli and Galeazzi let Pope Francis speak for himself, presenting here the full text of an interview with the pope precisely on his comments about the economy."

—Cindy Wooden
Rome Bureau Chief, Catholic News Service

"Tornielli and Galeazzi bring into focus one of Pope's Francis's fundamental concerns. They are meticulous in probing his writings and pronouncements on economic and financial matters, concern for the poor, defense of creation, and the big business of war. They also look seriously at the Pope's toughest critics. But the real value of this book is that Tornielli and Galeazzi bring us into an almost personal dialogue with Pope Francis—especially through an exclusive interview—and help us see how his authentic concern for all people, especially those who are poor and forgotten, is at the heart of his ministry."

—Robert Mickens
Editor, *Global Pulse Magazine*

"*This Economy Kills* provides a valuable window into Pope Francis's sophisticated understanding of Catholic social teaching, the economy, and the signs of the times."

—Meghan Clark
Author of *The Vision of Catholic Social Thought*

D1564832

"*This Economy Kills* settles an important question in the papacy of Pope Francis: are his radical economics in keeping with the tradition of the Church? And if so, why do they seem to cause such upset among American conservatives? For Tornielli and Galeazzi, veteran Vatican reporters, the answer is clear: Pope Francis's theology is absolutely in keeping with predecessors from the Desert Fathers to the most recent popes, and his economics represent the application of this timeless theology to our most pressing contemporary problems. Understanding Pope Francis's approach to modern economic ills will likely be key to understanding his papacy—but his contributions to global dialogue on poverty and inequality will be integral to galvanizing people worldwide for change. Tornielli and Galeazzi narrate these different aspects of Francis's message expertly, and their insights could not be more timely."

—Elizabeth Stoker Bruenig, *The New Republic*

This Economy Kills

*Pope Francis on Capitalism
and Social Justice*

Andrea Tornielli and
Giacomo Galeazzi

Translated by Demetrio S. Yocum

LITURGICAL PRESS
Collegeville, Minnesota

www.litpress.org

Original Italian edition:
Papa Francesco
Questa Economia Uccide
© 2015 Edizioni Piemme Spa
Milano - Italy
www.edizpiemme.it

Cover design by Stefan Killen Design. Cover photo: CNS photo/Paul Haring.

1   2   3   4   5   6   7   8   9

Library of Congress Control Number: 2015936995

ISBN 978-0-8146-4725-7   978-0-8146-4704-2 (ebook)

CONTENTS

Preface

IS THE POPE A MARXIST?

Francis, the Economy that "Kills," and the Catholic Amnesia

> *"When I give food to the poor, they call me a saint. But when I ask why the poor have no food, they call me a communist."*
>
> —Hélder Câmara, Archbishop of Recife

> Today we also have to say "thou shalt not" to an economy of exclusion and inequality. Such an economy kills. How can it be that it is not a news item when an elderly homeless person dies of exposure, but it is news when the stock market loses two points? . . .
>
> Some people continue to defend trickle-down theories which assume that economic growth, encouraged by a free market, will inevitably succeed in bringing about greater justice and inclusiveness in the world. This opinion, which has never been confirmed by the facts, expresses a crude and naïve trust in the goodness of those wielding economic power and in the sacralized workings of the prevailing economic system. Meanwhile, the excluded are still waiting.[1]

It took a few sentences, a handful of words, a few scant paragraphs in a large and complex document dedicated to evangelization, or rather to the "joy of the gospel." Pope Francis, eight months after his election to the papacy, after publishing the exhortation *Evangelii*

Gaudium, was branded a Marxist by conservative commentators from the United States. And some time later, *The Economist* even called him a follower of Lenin for his diagnosis of capitalism and imperialism. Jorge Maria Bergoglio, the Argentinian Jesuit, who—as superior of the Society of Jesus in his country and then as archbishop of Buenos Aires—was known for never having adopted certain extreme theses of liberation theology to the point of being accused of conservatism, found himself compared to the philosopher of Trier and to his many followers—including the architect of the Bolshevik revolution. But even more striking than the crude allegations of Marxism and Leninism are the criticisms and caveats on this issue that began before the publication of the pope's apostolic exhortation and have persisted ever since. This pope "speaks too much of the poor," the marginalized, the underprivileged. This "Latin American" pope does not know much about economics. This pope coming "from the end of the world" demonizes capitalism—that is, the only system that allows the poor to be less poor. Not only does this pope make politically incorrect decisions (as when he went to the island of Lampedusa to pray in front of the sea that had become the graveyard of thousands of migrants, desperately searching for hope in Europe, and who instead drowned off the coast of the island), but he also interferes in matters that are none of his business, thus revealing himself to be a "pauperist."[2] The Italian newspaper *Il Foglio,* which during Benedict XVI's pontificate was known as *Il Soglio* (The See of Peter), even went so far as to call the Argentinian pope's words "heretical" and find him "guilty" of referring to the poor and the suffering as "the flesh of Christ." This was after embracing and blessing, for an hour and in silence, seriously ill children and young people in Assisi.

However, what is most surprising is not so much the shallowness of the allegations, but rather the apparent oblivion in which a substantial part of the great tradition of the church has fallen—a tradition that spans the church fathers to the magisterium of Pope Pius XI, born Achille Ratti, hardly a modernist or progressive.

For certain establishments and in certain circles, it is acceptable to speak of the poor, as long as it is done infrequently and especially as long as it is done in ways that are welcome in certain spheres. A bit of charity mixed with good feelings is fine. It helps to appease the conscience. Just do not overdo it. And, above all, do not dare to question the system—a system that, according to many Catholics, is the best of all worlds for the marginalized because it teaches the "right" theories. The wealthier the rich become, the better it is for the poor. This system has even become dogma in some Catholic circles, like other truths of faith. As a certain adage goes: Christianity is freedom, freedom is free enterprise (and, therefore, capitalism); hence, capitalism is Christianity in action. And of course we should not quibble about the fact that we live in an economy that has little or nothing to do with capitalism, as its connection with the so-called "real economy" is almost nil. The financial bubble, speculation, the stock market indices, the fact that the oscillation of those indices can hurl entire populations below the poverty line as it suddenly pushes up the price of some raw materials—all these are realities that we are asked to accept in the same way as the "side effects" of the "smart" wars of this last generation. Not only do we have to accept them, we also have to stay silent. Dogma is dogma, and whoever calls it into question is, at best, an idealist—or, worse, a dissident. Yes, because even before the catastrophe of the economic and financial crisis of recent years, all that the church, and Catholics more generally, are allowed to do is to make some appeals for more ethics. True, finance needs ethics! Those who operate in those spheres ought to have well fixed in mind the principles of natural morality, better still, of Christian morals. Without ethics, the world, we can see it for ourselves, is falling apart. But be careful not to go any further. Never try to lift a finger or to say that the emperor is naked; never put into question the sustainability of the current system. Never wonder whether it is right that those who die of hunger or cold, whether in Africa or in the streets below our houses, make less news than when the stock market loses two points, as it has often been observed by the man who sits on the throne of Peter today. Then you are called a "Marxist," a "pauperist," a poor dreamer from the end of the world, who needs to be "catechized" by those who, here in the West, know everything of how the world and the church go, and are just waiting to be able to teach it to you.

That certain comments are made by financial commentators and journalists, or members of the tea party movement in the United States, is not surprising, and in fact does not surprise anyone. We could almost say that it is normal. Much more surprising, however, is that their comments are endorsed in some sectors of the Catholic world. The same sectors that in recent decades have been nothing short of selective in looking at the heritage of the church's magisterium, carefully picking and choosing what values to embrace also in the public arena. The issues of poverty, social justice, and marginalization, have become the competence of the "Catholic-communists" and the "pauperists," to use two denigratory labels. Or "statists," a label which in some circles defines those who still believe that politics should have a regulating and supervisory role, so that those who have less are protected. Thus, not only the theological value of love of the poor, as attested in Jesus' words, is ignored, but a whole tradition of social teaching is dismissed; a tradition that in past years had been far more extreme and radical on these issues than the feeble voice of some contemporary Catholic groups.

In this context, certain allusions and tones hit a wrong note, or are considered even subversive, as those in the following passage:

> Do you want to honor Christ's body? Then do not scorn him in his nakedness, nor honor him here in the church with silken garments while neglecting him outside where he is cold and naked. For he who said: "This is my body," and made it so by his words, also said: "You saw me hungry and did not feed me" and "inasmuch as you did not do it for the least of my brothers, you did not do it for me." What we do here in the church requires a pure heart, not special garments; what we do outside requires great dedication.
>
> Let us learn, therefore, to be men of wisdom and to honor Christ as he desires. For a person being honored finds greatest pleasure in the honor he desires, not in the honor we think best. Peter thought he was honoring Christ when he refused to let him wash his feet; but what Peter wanted was not truly an honor, quite the opposite! Give him the honor prescribed in his law by giving your riches to the poor. For God does not want golden vessels but golden hearts.

Or like this other one:

> In the first place, it is obvious that not only is wealth concentrated in our times but an immense power and despotic economic dictatorship is consolidated in the hands of a few, who often are not owners but only the trustees and managing directors of invested funds which they administer according to their own arbitrary will and pleasure. This dictatorship is being most forcibly exercised by those who, since they hold the money and completely control it, control credit also and rule the lending of money. Hence they regulate the flow, so to speak, of the life-blood whereby the entire economic system lives, and have so firmly in their grasp the soul, as it were, of economic life that no one can breathe against their will."

These words were written neither by liberation theologians from Latin America nor by their European inspirers. Neither were they written by heretical thinkers targeted by the former Holy Office for their revolutionary ideas. They are not an expression of postconciliar progressivism, Catholic communism, or theological "pauperism."[3] Nor are they words spoken by rebel Sandinista priests. The first is a quotation from a homily on the Gospel of Matthew by the church father St. John Chrysostom, also known as John of Antioch, second patriarch of Constantinople, who lived from 344 to 407 CE, is venerated as a saint by both Catholics and Orthodox, and is recognized as one of the thirty-five Doctors of the Church. The second is a quote from Pope Pius XI's encyclical *Quadragesimo Anno*, published during the Great Depression in 1931, in which the courageous pontiff from Brianza railed against the "deadly and accursed internationalism of finance or international imperialism."

Why do these words sound so upsetting, to the point of being considered, at least from an Italian political perspective, too far to the left even for today's leftists? Why do assessments as clear and precise as the one formulated in Pius XI's encyclical—albeit tied to a specific historical moment, but nevertheless clearly prophetic and very suitable also to the present situation—sound light-years away from the proliferation of words repeated by those who are engaged in politics on the basis of certain Catholic values and affiliations?

Why have so many experts, those engaged in the "defense of Christian values" in contemporary Italy after the end of the Christian Democratic party—the universal party of Italian Catholics built at the end of the war from the ashes of the People's Popular Party and active until the beginning of the 1990s—not been able to do anything more than to continue to propose new versions of the antiquated "Gentiloni Pact," thus completely conceding to certain other political parties in exchange for the promise that some values would not be put into question? Why has the tradition of the social teaching of the church, and of post-war political Catholicism, been so readily dismissed? What happened? What made the words of great saints and popes, certainly beyond any suspicion of Marxism, so upsetting to some contemporary Catholic groups?

These are some of the questions that emerge in light of the criticisms directed toward Pope Francis. His insistence on these issues, his repeating that the "protocol" on which we will be judged is to be found in Jesus' words in Matthew 25, and his reference to the poor as "flesh of Christ" has upset many. And they have angered not only some well-meaning proponents of a law-and-order type of religion but also some self-appointed teachers of orthodoxy, so well-informed and knowledgeable as to feel more than qualified to judge sarcastically every comma of the pope's magisterium. Francis's words have also questioned the supposed certainties of those who have grown up believing that to talk about fighting poverty—and to be concretely committed to end poverty—is essentially "not very Catholic." These are the same people who have been raised thinking that the fight against poverty is, after all, a pauperistic or old Marxist inclination. In other words, they think that the fight against poverty has to do with a certain ideology, a legacy of the last followers of Marx and communism, or something good only for Christian idealists out of touch with reality and still fascinated by wolves (strictly red) in sheep's clothing. In short, they see this fight against poverty as something good only for those poor dreamers of fair trade or ethical banks.

The impression that one gets from Francis's words is that one of the most important aspects of his pontificate will be decided on these issues. Another impression is that there are specific interests at work to make people believe that the discussion, debate, and at times the confrontation are on other issues—for example, on doctrinal matters. And so we squabble, counting on our fingers how many times the pope spoke of the defense of the life of the unborn, or taking account of the possibility, under certain conditions, of readmission of the divorced and remarried Catholics to the sacraments.

The fact that to the See of Peter has been elected a pope who has never professed the ideology of liberation theology but who knows firsthand the disasters of a certain type of capitalism has been extraordinary in itself. Many are troubled when Francis speaks so often of poverty and criticizes the idolatry of money on which our societies, with ever more limited sovereignty, seem increasingly founded. The extreme reaction with which certain circles, including Catholic ones, intervene to quell the debate and sometimes ridicule—for example, in the United States—bishops who dare to raise their voice on social issues, immigration, and poverty give a glimpse of the anxiety that possible change can create. An anxiety emerging from the election of a pope who is reaffirming the social doctrine of the church and whose words seem to call into question the supposed "holy alliance" with certain forms of capitalism, which many thought was by now indisputable.

What, then, do these allegations against the pope mean? What are the reasons for his interventions on these issues? And what does his biography, his episcopate in Buenos Aires—the capital of a country that has experienced a dramatic financial depression at the dawn of the third millennium—tell us? Do his words, and those of the social doctrine of the church, have something to say to our economic and financial systems? These are some of the questions that we seek to address in depth within the pages of this book. A book that, in our humble intent, attempts to open new questions rather than provide answers in the hope that the pope's words—here gathered and examined—will inspire everyone to question the world in which we live, its rules, and its systems; to ask what can concretely be done, without unrealistic utopian visions or old ideologies; and to try to change it at least a little—and perhaps for the better.

chapter 1

A POOR CHURCH FOR THE POOR

[The] preference for the poor . . . is an option, or a special form of primacy in the exercise of Christian charity, to which the whole tradition of the Church bears witness.

—John Paul II, *Sollicitudo Rei Socialis*

From the very first moments of the new pontificate the concern for the poor has been central. In fact, immediately after accepting his election, the new pope had to communicate his first decision as bishop of Rome: the chosen name as pope. An idea flashed through the mind of Jorge Mario Bergoglio, thanks to the embrace of a beloved friend.

The last poll of the day, in the late afternoon of that rainy March 13, 2013, was the decisive one. The cardinal archbishop of Buenos Aires had reached the two-thirds majority in the first vote of the afternoon, the fourth of the conclave. Then, a mistake slowed down the election: at the moment of opening the urn to scrutinize the paper ballots of the fifth vote, one of the scrutineers had found one ballot more than the number of the voting cardinals. Apparently, a cardinal did not realize that two ballots were stuck together, thus introducing two instead of one in the urn. It was decided to not count those ballots, but to immediately repeat the vote, exactly as required by the rules of the conclave. Thus, the new pope was elected on the sixth ballot, not the fifth.

While the votes were piling up, Bergoglio was supported by his friend, the Brazilian Cardinal Cláudio Hummes, who was sitting next to him. At 7:05 p.m.—the time was recorded by Cardinal Angelo Comastri—the cardinal, after answering "*acepto*" (I accept) to the question of the dean, said to the voting cardinals, "*Vocabor Franciscus*" (my name will be Francis).

Speaking with journalists three days later, the pope himself explained the choice of his name. It was the first time in two thousand years of church history that a successor of Peter chose to be called Francis, and since the evening of the election some were urging people not to consider the *Poverello* (little poor man) of Assisi as the true inspiration behind the choice.

"Some people wanted to know why the Bishop of Rome wished to be called Francis," said the new pope. "Some thought of Francis Xavier, Francis de Sales."[1] In fact, these were recurring interpretations advanced by those who considered it too odd that a Jesuit pope would take the name of the saint of the Franciscans. It was a decision, however, that did not mature on the basis of abstract reasoning, but as a consequence of the embrace of a dear friend.

"During the election, I was seated next to the Archbishop Emeritus of São Paulo and Prefect Emeritus of the Congregation for the Clergy, Cardinal Cláudio Hummes: a good friend, a good friend!" said the pope. "When things were looking dangerous, he encouraged me," he added, referring to the progressive and relentless increase of the votes for him. "And when the votes reached two thirds, there was the usual applause, because the pope has been elected. And he gave me a hug and a kiss, and said, 'Don't forget the poor!'"

"Those words," continued the pope,

> came to me: the poor, the poor. Then, right away, thinking of the poor, I thought of Francis of Assisi. Then, I thought of all the wars, as the votes were still being counted, and till the end of the count. Francis is also the man of peace. That is how the name came into my heart: Francis of Assisi. For me, he is the man of poverty, the man of peace, the man who loves and protects creation; these days we do not have a very good relationship with creation, do we? He is the man who gives us this spirit of peace, the poor man. . . . How I would like a Church which is poor and for the poor!

In continuity with his words and especially with his work during the episcopate in Buenos Aires, the attention for the poor has become the trademark of Francis's pontificate. And it is interesting to note that in Francis (as it was for then-Cardinal Bergoglio) this attention and this commitment have nothing to do with the old tools of ideology but are brought back to their original evangelical source. It is in this sense that we should also interpret the Argentine pope's spontaneous words spoken at the Vigil of Pentecost, which took place in St. Peter's Square in the late afternoon of Saturday, May 18, 2013, which was attended by members of several Catholic associations and movements.[2] On that occasion, Francesco responded to the questions that were asked by laypeople at the end of their own testimonies. One question was along these lines: "Holy Father, I would like to ask you how I, how we, can live as a poor Church and for the poor. How does a suffering person pose a question for our faith? What practical, effective contribution can all of us, as members of lay movements and associations, make to the Church and to society in order to address this grave crisis that is affecting public ethics, the model of development, politics, that is to say, a new way of being men and women?"

For the pope, this question about Christian witness and the contribution of Christians to a new developmental model is also very important.

"I shall return to the idea of 'witness,'" Francesco replied:

> First of all, living out the Gospel is the main contribution we can make. The Church is neither a political movement nor a well-organized structure. That is not what she is. We are not an NGO, and when the Church becomes an NGO she loses her salt, she has no savor, she is only an empty organization. We need cunning here, because the devil deceives us and we risk falling into the trap of hyper-efficiency. Preaching Jesus is one thing; attaining goals, being efficient is another. No, efficiency is a different value. Basically the value of the Church is living by the Gospel and witnessing to our faith. The Church is the salt of the earth, she is the light of the world. She is called to make present in society the leaven of the Kingdom of God and she does this primarily with her witness, the witness of brotherly love, of solidarity and of sharing with others.

"When you hear people saying," the pope continued, "that solidarity is not a value but a 'primary attitude' to be got rid of . . . this will not do! They are thinking of an efficiency that is purely worldly. Times of crisis, like the one we are living through—you said earlier that 'we live in a world of lies'—this time of crisis, beware, is not merely an economic crisis. It is not a crisis of culture. It is a human crisis: it is the human person that is in crisis! Man himself is in danger of being destroyed! But man is the image of God! This is why it is a profound crisis!"

"At this time of crisis," the pope added,

> we cannot be concerned solely with ourselves, withdrawing into loneliness, discouragement and a sense of powerlessness in the face of problems. Please do not withdraw into yourselves! This is a danger: we shut ourselves up in the parish, with our friends, within the movement, with the like-minded . . . but do you know what happens? When the Church becomes closed, she becomes an ailing Church, she falls ill! That is a danger. Nevertheless we lock ourselves up in our parish, among our friends, in our movement, with people who think as we do . . . but do you know what happens? When the Church is closed, she falls sick, she falls sick. Think of a room that has been closed for a year. When you go into it there is a smell of damp, many things are wrong with it. A Church closed in on herself is the same, a sick Church. The Church must step outside herself. To go where? To the outskirts of existence, whatever they may be, but she must step out. Jesus tells us: "Go into all the world! Go! Preach! Bear witness to the Gospel!"

The pope went on inviting all to go out into the world, despite the risks: "But what happens if we step outside ourselves?" he asked and then responded immediately after:

> The same as can happen to anyone who comes out of the house and onto the street: an accident. But I tell you, I far prefer a Church that has had a few accidents to a Church that has fallen sick from being closed. Go out, go out! Think of what the Book of Revelation says as well. It says something beautiful: that Jesus stands at the door and knocks, knocks to be let into our heart. This is the mean-

ing of the Book of Revelation. But ask yourselves this question: how often is Jesus inside and knocking at the door to be let out, to come out? And we do not let him out because of our own need for security, because so often we are locked into ephemeral structures that serve solely to make us slaves and not free children of God. In this "stepping out" it is important to be ready for encounter. For me this word is very important. Encounter with others.

The encounter with others is important, the pope added,

because faith is an encounter with Jesus, and we must do what Jesus does: encounter others. We live in a culture of conflict, a culture of fragmentation, a culture in which I throw away what is of no use to me, a culture of waste. Yet on this point, I ask you to think—and it is part of the crisis—of the elderly, who are the wisdom of a people, think of the children . . . the culture of waste! However, we must go out to meet them, and with our faith we must create a "culture of encounter," a culture of friendship, a culture in which we find brothers and sisters, in which we can also speak with those who think differently, as well as those who hold other beliefs, who do not have the same faith. They all have something in common with us: they are images of God, they are children of God. Going out to meet everyone, without losing sight of our own position.

Then, Francis called attention to poverty, the presence of the poor in our cities:

There is another important point: encountering the poor. If we step outside ourselves we find poverty. Today—it sickens the heart to say so—the discovery of a tramp who has died of the cold is not news. Today what counts as news is, maybe, a scandal. A scandal: ah, that is news! Today, the thought that a great many children do not have food to eat is not news. This is serious, this is serious! We cannot put up with this! Yet that is how things are. We cannot become starched Christians, those over-educated Christians who speak of theological matters as they calmly sip their tea. No! We must become courageous Christians and go in search of the people who are the very flesh of Christ, those who are the flesh of Christ!

To go out in search of the poor means to go to the very flesh of Christ. Pope Francis cited an example from his experience as a confessor:

> When I go to hear confessions—I still can't, because to go out to hear confessions . . . from here it's impossible to go out, but that's another problem—when I used to go to hear confessions in my previous diocese, people would come to me and I would always ask them: "Do you give alms?"—"Yes, Father!" "Very good." And I would ask them two further questions: "Tell me, when you give alms, do you look the person in the eye?" "Oh I don't know, I haven't really thought about it." The second question: "And when you give alms, do you touch the hand of the person you are giving them to or do you toss the coin at him or her?" This is the problem: the flesh of Christ, touching the flesh of Christ, taking upon ourselves this suffering for the poor. Poverty for us Christians is not a sociological, philosophical or cultural category, no. It is theological. I might say this is the first category, because our God, the Son of God, abased himself, he made himself poor to walk along the road with us. This is our poverty: the poverty of the flesh of Christ, the poverty that brought the Son of God to us through his Incarnation.

The concern for the poor is, therefore, not the result of ideological positions and sociological analyses, nor the outcome of a political decision or of a project to change society straight off the drawing board. Francis reconnects this commitment to its original evangelical roots, that is, Jesus' words. For Christians, it is not an option at all but has to do with faith itself.

"A poor church for the poor," explained Francis during that same vigil of Pentecost,

> begins by reaching out to the flesh of Christ. If we reach out to the flesh of Christ, we begin to understand something, to understand what this poverty, the Lord's poverty, actually is; and this is far from easy. However, there is one problem that can afflict Christians: the spirit of the world, the worldly spirit, spiritual worldliness. This leads to self-sufficiency, to living by the spirit

of the world rather than by the spirit of Jesus. You asked the question: how should we live in order to address this crisis that affects public ethics, the model of development and politics? Since this is a crisis of man, a crisis that destroys man, it is a crisis that strips man of ethics. In public life, in politics, if there is no ethics, an ethics of reference, everything is possible and everything can be done. We see, moreover, whenever we read the newspapers, that the lack of ethics in public life does great harm to the whole of humanity.

Then, the pope recounted an old anecdote, capable of describing the current reality:

I would like to tell you a story. I have already told it twice this week, but I will tell it a third time to you. It is taken from a biblical *midrash* by a 12th-century rabbi. He tells the tale of the building of the Tower of Babel and he says that, in order to build the Tower of Babel, bricks had to be made. What does this mean? Going out and mixing the mud, fetching straw, doing everything . . . then the kiln. And when the brick was made it had to be hoisted, for the construction of the Tower of Babel. Every brick was a treasure because of all the work required to make it. Whenever a brick fell, it was a national tragedy and the guilty workman was punished; a brick was so precious that if it fell there was a great drama. Yet if a workman fell, nothing happened, that was something else. This happens today: if the investments in the banks fall slightly . . . a tragedy . . . what can be done? But if people die of hunger, if they have nothing to eat, if they have poor health, it does not matter! This is our crisis today! And the witness of a poor Church for the poor goes against this mentality.

chapter 2

THE IMPERIALISM OF MONEY

> *In any case we clearly see, and on this there is general agreement,*
> *that some opportune remedy must be found quickly for the misery*
> *and wretchedness pressing so unjustly on the majority of the*
> *working class. . . . By degrees it has come to pass that working men*
> *have been surrendered, isolated and helpless, to the hardheartedness*
> *of employers and the greed of unchecked competition.*
>
> —Leo XIII, *Rerum Novarum*

Although chosen "from the end of the world" at the time of his election, Jorge Mario Bergoglio had behind him twenty years of episcopacy in the megalopolis of Buenos Aires, the capital of Argentina. A remote megacity, far away from Europe, characterized by phenomena, processes, challenges, and problems that put it "at the margins," but at the same time at the "heart" of the world—even from the perspective of the global socio-economic challenges and contradictions. At the beginning of the new millennium, the large South American country experienced an economic-financial collapse. In December 2001, the country was wrecked by severe social unrest. Many families ended up on the streets. One day, from a window of the archbishop's residence, Bergoglio, who had recently been appointed cardinal, saw the police in the Plaza de Mayo charging a woman. The archbishop picked up the telephone and called the minister of the interior. They did not put him through but had him speak instead to the secretary of security. The archbishop asked whether he knew the difference between agitprop and people who were simply asking to get their own money back, which was being held by the banks. The future pope spoke of his own experience during those months in a long interview with Gianni Valente, published in the journal *30Giorni*, in January 2002.[1]

"The image of the depression that Cardinal Jorge Mario Bergoglio always has in his mind," wrote the journalist introducing the interview, "is not the noisy, angry *cacerolazo* street protest, but the intimate one, the image of battered dignity, of mothers and fathers who weep in the night when their children are asleep, when no one can see them. 'They cry like babies, like the babies they were when their own mothers would have used to comfort them. Their only consolation are God our Lord and his Mother.'"

"In the presence of a people strangled by the anonymous, perverse mechanisms of speculative economy," Valente observed, "even he, usually a quiet and reserved man, becomes severe."

Bergoglio cited the "Letter to the People of God," written by the Argentinian Episcopal Conference and published on November 17, 2001, which described "many aspects of this unprecedented crisis: the concept of the state as something magical; the squandering of the people's money; the extreme liberalism wielded by the tyrannical market; tax evasion; lack of respect for the law, as much in the way it is set down and applied as in terms of observance; the loss of a work ethic; in short, a generalized corruption that undermines the cohesion of the nation and takes away its prestige in the eyes of the world. This is the diagnosis. In the final analysis, the root of the Argentinian depression is of the moral order."

Far from being a mishap, although of enormous proportions, the Argentinian depression seemed rather a crisis of the system, of the economic model imposed on the country over the previous two decades. The words of the then-cardinal of Buenos Aires were explicit:

> Throughout this time, there has been economic financial terrorism proper. And it has had its consequences which are not hard to see: more rich people, more poor people, and a drastically

reduced middle class. There have been other less circumstantial consequences, such as the disaster in the field of education. At this moment in the city of Buenos Aires and in its residential suburbs, there are two million young people who neither study nor work. Given the barbarous form assumed by the financial globalization in Argentina, the church in this country has always taken the indications contained in the magisterium as its points of reference. They are for example, the criteria outlined in no uncertain terms in John Paul II's allocution, *Ecclesia in America*.

"Seventy years ago, in the encyclical *Quadragesimo Anno*, written just after the Wall Street Crash of 1929, Pius XI had described the speculative economic model with the power to impoverish millions of families from one minute to the next as 'the international imperialism of money.'"

A forgotten expression of Pius XI, Bergoglio considered this phrase timely to describe the situation of the depression in Argentina:

> It's a definition that never loses its pertinence, and it has a biblical root. When Moses went up to the mountain to receive God's law, the people became guilty of idolatry in fabricating the golden calf. Today's imperialism of money also has an unequivocal idolatrous face. It is curious how idolatry always goes hand in glove with gold. And where there is idolatry, God and the dignity of man made in God's image are cancelled. So the new imperialism of money even takes work away, which is the one expression of the dignity of man, of his creativity, the image of God's own creativity. The speculative economy does not even have any further need of labor. It bows down to the idol of cash which is self-generating. This is why there is no remorse in turning millions of workers out of their jobs.

This is the description of a reality, of processes at work, felt and experienced by a man who at the time was the pastor of the diocese of Buenos Aires. Bergoglio explained how the church looked at that phenomenon without falling into the trap of ideology, but at the same time without ending up justifying—in the name of the fight against ideology—profoundly unjust models.

"The Puebla documents," explained the future pope,

> are important on this point. The Latin American Episcopal Council meeting in Puebla was a watershed. They managed to look at Latin America through dialogue with its own cultural tradition. And likewise as regards the political and economic systems, the good things they were concerned about were the religious and spiritual resources of our peoples, expressed in the grassroots religious sense, for example, that Paul VI in his time had exalted in his apostolic letter *Evangelii Nuntiandi*, no. 48. The Christian experience is not an ideological one. Its distinguishing feature is originality which is not negotiable, which is born of the wonder of the encounter with Jesus Christ, of one's wonder at the person of Jesus Christ. And this is kept up by our people, is manifest in grassroots devotions. The leftist ideologies and this now triumphant economic imperialism of money all cancel this Christian originality of the encounter with Jesus Christ, which is still part of the lives of so many of our people in their simplicity of faith.

In that interview, Cardinal Bergoglio addressed the role played by the international community and central financial organizations in the Argentinian depression: "I don't think that man is central to their thinking, despite all the fine things they say. They always recommend governments to adopt their rigid directives, always talk about ethics and transparency, but they seem to me to be 'ethicalistic' only, devoid of goodness."

And regarding the church's criteria in taking action during that time, he added: "In involving ourselves in the common effort to find a way out of the depression in Argentina we keep in mind what the tradition of the church teaches. A tradition that describes the oppression of the poor and the act of defrauding workers of their wages as two sins that cry to God for vengeance. These two traditional formulas are totally pertinent to the magisterium of the Argentinian Episcopate. We are tired of systems that generate poor people for the church then to look after."

"Only 40 percent," explained Bergoglio, "of the resources designated to the most needy sectors by the state ever reach them. The rest get lost along the way. There is corruption. The church has launched an extensive parochial network of canteens for the increasing numbers of children and adults living on the streets."

And at a moment when the country's leadership and managerial classes had been totally discredited, the future pope reaffirmed the importance of politics and political commitment. "The important role of politics must be restored however much the politicians have discredited it; as Paul VI said, politics can be one of the highest forms of charity. In our country, for example, the 'functionalist' approach associated with the dominant economic model experimented with the two extreme phases of life, children and the elderly, the two age groups worst hit by the crisis because of the devastation it has caused in the fields of education, health, and social assistance. A people that does not look after its children and elderly is a people without hope."

Archbishop Bergoglio's closeness to his people, especially the poor, the weak, and the sick, was the hallmark of his episcopate. He celebrated many Masses among the *cartoneros* (collectors of cardboard from waste fields), in the *villas miserias* (slums in Buenos Aires), and among the unemployed. He was always close to the church that is on the "frontier," sending priests to the *villas miserias*, caring for their training, encouraging and supporting them, and especially visiting them.

As archbishop, Bergoglio used strong words to define some problematic aspects of the reality of Argentinian megacities: "In Buenos Aires, slavery has not been abolished. Here there are people who still work as if they were slaves," he once said before the members of the NGO La Alameda, a group of activists against the trafficking of women for sexual purposes and against the slave-like working conditions of the many illegal textile *atelier* and seasonal workers arriving from neighboring countries for the harvest season or fruit picking.

During the conference of the Latin American bishops in Aparecida, a meeting in which Bergoglio had a significant role, particularly in preparing the final document, the then-cardinal archbishop of Buenos Aires spoke of inequalities and distribution of wealth that produces "a scandalous inequality." It was May 16, 2007. With reference to the social dimension, Bergoglio spoke of a "scandalous inequality affecting personal dignity and social justice." Discussing the specific situation of Argentina, he observed:

> Between 2002 and 2006, the poverty rate in Argentina rose by 8.7 percent; it currently is at 26.9 percent, and apparently we are in the most unequal region in the world, the one that grew the most but also the one that reduced poverty the least. The unjust distribution of goods persists, which creates a situation of social sin that cries to heaven and excludes many brothers and sisters from the chances of a fuller life. Political powers and economic plans of different types show no sign of producing significant changes to "eliminate the structural causes of global economic dysfunction" (Benedict XVI, Address to the Diplomatic Corps, January 8, 2007). In Argentina it is urgent to promote a just conduct, consistent with a faith that promotes human dignity, the common good, full inclusion, full citizenship, and the rights of the poor.

Worth noting in the passage quoted here is the contradiction inherent in the theory that economic growth always brings about opportunities for enrichment for all people. When, as we will see, in the exhortation *Evangelii Gaudium*, Pope Francis challenges the "trickle-down" economic theory, it will not be on the basis of opposite theories but by virtue of his experience observing the situation of the Argentinian people, in a country where high growth rates were accompanied by an increase in poverty rates. Worth noting also is the future pope's reference, drawing on a speech by Pope Benedict XVI, to "the structural causes" of this situation.

Bergoglio reiterated the same points in 2011, at the Congress of the Social Doctrine held in Argentina. On that occasion, the cardinal criticized "an economy that offers almost unlimited possibilities in all aspects of life to those who manage to be included in that system."

During the twenty years of his episcopacy in Argentina, Bergoglio's public positions on the issues of social justice and concern for the poor have always been traced to their evangelical root. This aspect becomes clear especially during an intervention that the then-cardinal archbishop of Buenos Aires recorded to be broadcast during Argentina's national Caritas meeting, in 2009.

Bergoglio on that occasion began with an example:

> At a Caritas center things happen that should not happen . . . .
> Excuse me if I offend any of you; I do not mean to offend any-
> one. I just want you all to understand the dangers of today in
> promoting charity in the church. At one of the centers a party
> was thrown for one of the coworkers. The party took place in
> one of the 36 luxury restaurants of Puerto Madero in Buenos
> Aires, where the most economic dinner costs 250 pesos. These
> 36 restaurants are only within a mile from a shack of one of
> the *villas miserias*. If you want to share in Caritas's mission of
> solidarity with the poor, your habits must change accordingly.
> You cannot afford certain luxuries that you used to enjoy before
> your conversion. You may say, 'Father, you are a Communist!'
> Maybe, but I don't think so! I only interpret what the church asks
> of each one of us. To work with Caritas means to renounce to
> something. It requires spiritual poverty. Solidarity has to take you
> to the visible gesture of spiritual poverty. "The Latin American
> Church is called to be a sacrament of love, solidarity, and justice
> within our peoples (*Aparecida Document*, 396)."

Archbishop Bergoglio insisted on personal commitment and
change in the personal lives of those who are involved in helping the poor:

> When you live charity in this way, your life is under renovation,
> your flesh is changing. You are the one who becomes poor in a way
> and rich in others. Caritas service must lead to a radical change
> of lifestyle. Many years ago, it was with shame that we attended
> luxury dinners to raise money for Caritas. Jewelry was auctioned—
> expensive stuff. You were wrong! That was not Caritas! That is
> an NGO. With Aparecida we are in front of a choice of the heart:
> either you are part of an NGO, or of Caritas. If you become part of
> the latter, let your life be changed. Your lifestyle will be changed
> anyway. You will become a friend of the poor and you yourself will
> become poor, in the austere modesty of your new life."

The future pope then referred to *Mafalda*, a popular Argenti-
anian comic strip character created by Quino (the pseudonym of

the Argentine cartoonist Joaquín Salvador Lavado). "But if you want to do good in an NGO," Bergoglio added, "maybe you'll end up like Susanita, Mafalda's friend, who once said: 'When I grow up, I will organize tea parties with cookies and classy stuff, so then I can buy polenta, pasta, and the other junk the poor eat.' When you enter into the dynamics of conversion, of a life conversion, of solidarity to the flesh of your brothers and sisters, when you are not ashamed of them, then the horizon widens up for you and you will see Jesus' face. And the contemplation in seeking the face of God in the poor, becomes the contemplation of the face of Jesus himself. But for this to happen, we need much prayer."

"Caritas workers give hope," explained Cardinal Bergoglio,

> because they themselves have already been filled with the hope of Christ who was close to the weak and the poor. "The church is called to be the advocate of justice and of the poor in the face of intolerable social and economic inequalities which cry to heaven" (*Aparecida Document*, 395). The social doctrine of the church is capable of inspiring hope in the midst of the most difficult situations because if there is no hope for the poor, then there is no hope for anyone, not even for the rich. If you are unable to offer hope to the poor, then you yourself will be without. You will live for the day, for daily contentment, filling your time with small gratifications . . . with no horizons. You will be a Christian of circumstance, making sure that you do not lack anything.

The future pope continued by mentioning the "unjust structures" and the commitment to change them—a commitment that is not based on ideological positions but represents the horizon of the Christian who is close to the poor.

> The preferential option for the poor demands that we proclaim this truth to our leaders to change unjust structures. In doing so, it also asks that they themselves become open to hope. Many men and women engaged in social work do not know the meaning of what the church calls social justice. The social doctrine of the church opens up the horizon starting from the poor you have come to know, helped, and accompanied. Then you even

start to love them. And then, you start to enter into their lives and they in yours. You start to include them, thus opening up the horizon of hope. You give hope to them, and they give it back to you. Justice opens you to the mission of giving hope to those in charge, to change the nature of social structures. We must not forget what Pope Benedict XVI said: "For the Church, the service of charity, like the proclamation of the Word and celebration of the sacraments, is an indispensable expression of her very being" (*Aparecida Document*, 399). Do not think that you are a good Catholic just because you go to Church, you go often to confession, and do some charity work, collaborating with Caritas, but then you keep living according to the spirit of the world. Aparecida asks us to give up all worldliness, that is, to give up the spirit of the world, the same one that did not welcome Jesus. Your renunciation creates space in you for Jesus' wonderful revelation; a beautiful face hidden in the dirty and wounded faces of the many men and women of this world.

In October 2009, Bergoglio spoke about the social debt at the opening of a seminar on the topic: "The ethical foundation from which we must judge the social debt as immoral, unjust, and illegitimate is the social recognition of the serious damage that its effects have on life, on the value of life, and therefore on human dignity."

"The greatest immorality," continued Bergoglio, referring to a ruling of the Argentinian bishops "lies in the fact that it happens in a nation that has the objective conditions for avoiding or correcting such harm, but unfortunately it seems that the same country opts for exacerbating inequalities even more. This debt involves those who have the moral or political responsibility to protect and promote the dignity of the people and their rights, and those parts of society whose rights are violated."

"Human rights," concluded Bergoglio, citing the Santo Domingo document of the Latin American Bishops, "are violated not only by terrorism, repression, and murders, but also by the existence of conditions of extreme poverty and unjust economic structures that cause great inequalities."

Finally, we would be remiss if we did not mention Bergoglio's Lenten message, his last as archbishop of Buenos Aires. On that occasion, the cardinal urged to produce "a change" in Argentinian society, warning his fellow citizens of the risk of getting used to living under the effects of the "dominance of money," whose "demonic effects" are "drugs, corruption, the trafficking of persons, including children," and "violence that kills and destroys families."[2]

"Little by little we get used to hearing and seeing, through the media, the crime news in contemporary society, presented almost with perverse enjoyment; and yet, we get used to it, and we live with violence that kills, destroys families, and rekindles wars and conflicts."

"The suffering of the innocent and non-violent never ceases to hit us; contempt for the rights of the most vulnerable individuals and peoples is not unknown to us: the empire of money with its demonic effects such as drugs, corruption, human trafficking, including children, along with poverty, both material and moral, are the common currency." After stating that "the destruction of dignified work, the painful migrations, and the lack of a future are also part of this symphony," Bergoglio admitted that "not even our mistakes and sins as Church remain outside this general panorama."

"Today we are again invited to undertake a paschal journey toward life, a path that includes the cross and renunciation, which will be painful but not sterile. We are invited to admit that something is not right in ourselves, in society, and in the Church; we are invited to change, to turn around, to be converted."

Bergoglio continued by saying: "The most personal egoisms are justified, the lack of ethical values in a society that metastasizes in families, in the environment of neighborhoods, in towns and cities, testify to our limitations, our weakness, and our inability to transform this long list of destructive realities."

In the face of this situation, Bergoglio also recognized: "The trap of impotence that makes one think if it is worth trying to change when the world continues its carnival dance disguising for a while everything." But the future pope recalled that "when the mask falls, the truth appears." Finally, Archbishop Bergoglio invited his audience to have hope, pointing out that, beyond the plastic smiles and applications of makeup, Lent represents the possibility of real change. And this liturgical time "is not only for us, but also for the transformation of our families, our communities, our Church, our country, and the whole world." Lent is an opportunity "that God gives us to grow and mature in our encounter with the Lord who is made visible in the face of the suffering of so many children without a future, in the trembling hands of the elderly who have been forgotten, in the feeble knees of many families" who face life "without finding anyone to assist them."

chapter 3

THE GLOBALIZATION OF INDIFFERENCE

The hungry nations of the world cry out to the peoples blessed with abundance. And the Church, cut to the quick by this cry, asks each and every man to hear his brother's plea and answer it lovingly.

—Paul VI, *Populorum Progressio*

The Arena sporting field, in Salina on the island of Lampedusa, is a "non-place" that gives one chills. Next to the vacationers are the wretched boat people. Francis's first travel as pope was to this island, which marks the Italian border in the far south of the country. The trip was planned in no time. The pope was struck by yet more news of deaths at sea: men, women, and children crammed on a boat that sank before they could have reached the European shores. Thus, Bergoglio decided to come here on July 8, 2013, without the retinue of national and local politicians, without much authority in tow.

Francis's face was grave while talking under a harsh sun. Unbridled capitalism is like Herod who "sowed death to defend his own well-being, his own soap bubble. And so it continues." Francis's words sounded like a warning to the globalized society of the third millennium.[1]

"Let us ask the Lord to remove the part of Herod that lurks in our hearts; let us ask the Lord for the grace to weep over our indifference, to weep over the cruelty of our world, of our own hearts, and of all those who in anonymity make social and economic decisions which open the door to tragic situations like this."

"Has any one wept?" is the question that the pope repeated while thinking about those dead whose tomb is now in the depths of the sea. "Today has anyone wept in our world?" The pope, who wants a poor church for the poor, asks forgiveness for our indifference toward so many brothers and sisters: "Father, we ask your pardon for those who are complacent and closed amid comforts which have deadened their hearts; we beg your forgiveness for those who by their decisions on the global level have created situations that lead to these tragedies. Forgive us, Lord!"

Lampedusa is an island, but it is also a beacon: "May this example be a beacon that shines throughout the world, so that people will have the courage to welcome those in search of a better life." A beacon for all, exhorting us to become missionaries in our home countries: "Immigrants dying at sea, in boats which were vehicles of hope and became vehicles of death," said Francis in one of the most powerful homilies in his first year of pontificate. "So I felt that I had to come here today, to pray and to offer a sign of my closeness, but also to challenge our consciences lest this tragedy be repeated. . . .

"'Adam, where are you?' This is the first question which God asks man after his sin. 'Adam, where are you?' Adam lost his bearings, his place in creation, because he thought he could be powerful, able to control everything, to be God. Harmony was lost; man erred and this error occurs over and over again also in relationships with others. 'The other' is no longer a brother or sister to be loved, but simply someone who disturbs my life and my comfort. God asks," continued the pope, "a second question: 'Cain, where is your brother?' The illusion of being powerful, of being as great as God, even of being God himself, leads to a whole series of errors, a chain of death, even to the spilling of a brother's blood!"

The visit to Lampedusa was a pilgrimage at sea; it marked Francis's first official trip out of Rome. Francis's debut was a surprise visit to the poor that somehow bypassed and disoriented the Vatican Curia machine, and it inaugurated a pontificate "on the road." Just a week before, the announcement had come from the Vatican press office; without mediation of the Secretariat of State, Francis had confirmed directly to the archbishop of Agrigento, Francesco Montenegro, that he had accepted the invitation from the pastor of Lampedusa, Don Stefano Nastasi. The official authorities of the Italian state and the Italian Episcopal Conference (CEI) were not included in the program. The first pope to visit Lampedusa, Francis's whirlwind trip was to remember the many migrants who lost their lives at sea, between Africa and Lampedusa, victims of war profiteers and smugglers. This trip was to encourage solidarity among the people of Lampedusa, and to appeal to the responsibility of all to assist the migrants.

"It is a significant gesture that shakes the indifference of the institutions toward these tragedies at sea," said the president of the Pontifical Council for the Pastoral Care of Migrants and Itinerants, Cardinal Antonio Maria Vegliò, shortly after the announcement of the trip. Two months before flying to Lampedusa, Francis had launched an appeal to governments, legislators, and the international community to face the reality of migrants and refugees "with effective initiatives and new approaches to protect their dignity, improve their quality of life, and meet the challenges that emerge from modern forms of persecution, oppression, and slavery."

The initiative to make a significant gesture in favor of immigrants and refugees had come from the "recent sinking of a boat," in mid-June, an event that "deeply touched" the pope. Francis's visit to Lampedusa was sober. The fishermen accompanied the pope offshore with their boats where a wreath was launched into the sea in memory of the many victims.

Later, Francis celebrated Mass in a sports field and then stopped for a short visit at the local parish of St. Gerlando. With only his presence, even before any speech or remark, Francis turned the spotlight on places that have become the theater of daily dramas and tragic stories, but also of hope and solidarity. "Francis's choice to go to Lampedusa as the first trip of his pontificate speaks more than any words," stressed the Vatican's daily newspaper *L'Osservatore Romano*.

In our global era, where apparently there are no more geopolitical barriers, Pope Francis visited the outpost of charity, the first front line in a war for survival fought every night on tramp steamers. It was a pilgrimage to an island that only in 2011, with the explosion of the Arab Spring, saw fifty thousand people landing on its shores. The president of the *Migrantes* foundation, Fr. Giancarlo Perego, pointed out that the pope's visit to Lampedusa reiterated "the preferential option for the poor of the church." The last shipwreck prompted the pope to go to the door of Europe. A journey that in itself is an encyclical. On this island of tears, Francis placed everyone, absolutely everyone, in front of their responsibilities. He spoke as bishop, questioning the consciences of the indifferent ones, and was informed of everyday details of the life of immigrants in the islands' welcoming centers.

It was a short visit of just four hours, but it was full of meaning. Pope Francis begged God's forgiveness for having ignored this "massacre of the innocents": 25,000 dead in twenty years.

Shocked by the stories of the shipwreck survivors, the pope, himself a son of migrants, interrupted his homily in the stadium and condemned smugglers and traffickers for the exploitation of the 100 million people in the world who every year are forced to leave their homes for political or economic reasons, or for wars and conflicts. He turned to those "who are complacent and closed amid comforts which have deadened their hearts." He passed in front of the cemetery of the boat people and called for the "courage to welcome those in search of a better life." Wearing purple vestments (as a sign of penance) and with biblical references to Herod and God's questions to Adam and Cain, the pope condemned the fracture in the "relationships" because of "my comfort." He described the mistakes of "a chain of death, even to the spilling of a brother's blood." Referencing the famous Italian novel, *The Betrothed,* Pope Francis asserted that the "globalization of indifference" turns all of us into "Manzoni's character—'the Unnamed,'" and reduces our lives to a "soap bubble."

Thus, "we see our brother half dead on the side of the road, and perhaps we say to ourselves: 'poor soul!' and then go on our way." "A society that has forgotten how to weep, how to experience compassion" raises walls of selfishness. For these brothers and sisters, he asked, "has anyone wept in our world?"

Francis was clear: "God will judge us based on how we treated the migrants." Even St. Francis was an illegal immigrant; after his conversion, as a pilgrim in Syria, he secretly boarded a ship. Pope Francis's first trip outside Rome was a "business trip" that seemed like more of a social encyclical. His words made a deep impression on the inhabitants of Lampedusa: "How many of us, myself included, have lost our bearings; we are no longer attentive to the world in which we live; we don't care; we don't protect what God created for everyone, and we end up unable even to care for one another! And when humanity as a whole loses its bearings, it results in tragedies like the one we have witnessed."

"In Spanish literature," recalled the pope, "we have a comedy of Lope de Vega which tells how the people of the town of Fuente Ovejuna kill their governor because he is a tyrant. They do it in such a way that no one knows who the actual killer is. So when the royal judge asks: 'Who killed the governor?', they all reply: 'Fuente Ovejuna, sir.' Everybody and nobody! Today too, the question has to be asked: Who is responsible for the blood of these brothers and sisters of ours? Nobody! That is our answer: It isn't me; I don't have anything to do with it; it must be someone else, but certainly not me. Yet God is asking each of us: 'Where is the blood of your brother which cries out to me?'"

Therefore, we live in a "culture of comfort, which makes us think only of ourselves, makes us insensitive to the cries of other people, makes us live in soap bubbles which, however lovely, are insubstantial; they offer a fleeting and empty illusion which results in indifference to others; indeed, it even leads to the globalization of indifference. In this globalized world, we have fallen into globalized indifference. We have become used to the suffering of others: it doesn't affect me; it doesn't concern me; it's none of my business!"

On September 22, 2013, Pope Francis arrived in Sardinia, the Italian island marked by unemployment. He was wearing the helmet of the workers of Alcoa and chanting "work, work, work" together with the 350,000 faithful who for the whole day hailed him as the voice of the island's distress, while booing and protesting against politicians and authorities.[2] Francis spoke of labor as a source of dignity and life and against the power groups that, having no interest in the common good, have caused the global economic crisis. The pope speaks of work for everyone, but work that is dignified, not slave labor, and one that safeguards rest and God's creation. Work was the pope's key point on his trip to Cagliari, Sardinia's capital, prompted by the island's dramatic economic situation where the index of relative poverty is twice the national average; half of the young people are jobless, and requests for help for food, and money to pay bills, including energy bills to stay warm, at Caritas centers have increased exponentially. "Francis is not stealing the spotlight from us trade unionists; rather, he is strengthening our battle with Alcoa as in many other plants," said the secretary of CISL, the Italian Confederation of Workers' Trade Unions, Raffaele Bonanni. "Now no one can say they did not know. The pope has years of experience of social injustice in Latin America, and his economic analysis is impeccable. Without tackling the causes (services, bureaucracy, infrastructure, energy costs), there is no escape from the crisis: Francis remains the only global authority to counter the monstrous mechanism that is turning labor into a commodity and sowing rubbles in national democracies."

On the pope's agenda, there was already a call for labor reform, for a solution to the crisis that is not welfare, but that restores energy and hope to people. But when the pope heard three testimonies (of a worker unemployed since 2009, a co-op entrepreneur, and a shepherd) a cry of alarm came from his heart. When Francesco Mattana, unemployed since 2008, cited two colleagues who died at work, Francis was moved. He completely abandoned his prepared speech and spoke spontaneously; not as a "Church employee" who says "be brave" and then goes back home, but "as a pastor, as a man" who wants to participate and fight together for a just system, to move forward together for work and dignity, against an economic system that worships money and discards people, young and old, throwing away those who are considered useless.

"With this visit," said the pope, "I am starting with you, who make up the world of work. With this meeting I want above all to express my closeness to you, especially to the situations of suffering: to the many young people out of work, to people on unemployment benefits, or on a temporary basis, to business and tradespeople who find it hard to keep going."

Regarding the experience of unemployment and of crisis, Francis recalled that "I myself was spared it but my family wasn't. My father went to Argentina as a young man full of illusions 'of making it in America.' And he suffered in the dreadful recession of the 1930s. They lost everything! There was no work! And in my childhood I heard talk of this period at home. . . . I never saw it, I had not yet been born, but I heard about this suffering at home, I heard talk of it. I know it well!"

The pope's words, however, were of hope and encouragement: "I must say to you: 'Courage!' Nevertheless I am also aware that for my own part I must do everything to ensure that this term 'courage' is not a beautiful word spoken in passing! May it not be merely the smile of a courteous employee, a Church employee who comes and says 'be brave!' No! I don't want this! I want courage to come from within me and to impel me to do everything as a pastor, as a man. We must all face this challenge with solidarity, among you—also among us—we must all face with solidarity and intelligence this historic struggle."

Francis then recalled that Cagliari is the second Italian city that he had visited. And both are on islands. In the first, in Lampedusa, "I saw the suffering of so many people on a quest, risking their life, their dignity, their livelihood, their health: the world of refugees. And I saw the response of that city which—as an island—did not want to isolate itself and receives them, makes them its own. It gives us an example of hospitality: suffering meets with a positive response. In this second city, an island that I am visiting, I here too find suffering. Suffering which, as one of you has said, 'weakens you and ends by robbing you of hope.' It is a form of suffering, the shortage of work—that leads you—excuse me if I am coming over a little strong but I am telling the truth—to feel that you are deprived of dignity! Where there is no work there is no dignity! And this is not only a problem in Sardinia—but it is serious here!—it is not only a problem in Italy or in certain European countries, it is the result of a global decision, of an economic system which leads to this tragedy; an economic system centred on an idol called 'money.'"

Francis's words were simple and direct. This situation was the result of a "world choice," a system that worships money. It is caused by the excessive power of finance under which the world has been living for decades. But Francis warned that

> God did not want an idol to be at the centre of the world but man, men and women who would keep the world going with their work. Yet now, in this system devoid of ethics, at the centre there is an idol and the world has become an idolater of this "god-money." Money is in command! Money lays down the law! It orders all these things that are useful to it, this idol. And what happens? To defend this idol all crowd to the centre and those on the margins are done down, the elderly fall away, because there is no room for them in this world! Some call this habit "hidden euthanasia," not caring for them, not taking them into account. . . . "No, let's not bother about them." And the young who do not find a job collapse, and their dignity with them.

A world where young people, rather two generations of young people, have no work, is a world that

> has no future. Why? Because they have no dignity! It is hard to have dignity without work. This is your difficulty here. This is the prayer you were crying out from this place: "work," "work," "work." It is a necessary prayer. Work means dignity, work means taking food home, work means loving! To defend this idolatrous economic system the "culture of waste" has become established; grandparents are thrown away and young people are thrown away. And we must say "no" to this "culture of waste." We must say "we want a just system! A system that enables everyone to get on." We must say: "we don't want this globalized economic system which does us so much harm!" Men and women must be at the centre as God desires, and not money!

So it is not only the sin, the lack of ethics, and the idolatry of money of a single individual. "We do not want a system" that focuses on money and not on men and women, the pope said, referring to the pronouncements of the social doctrine of the church.

"But to all, to you all," said Francis,

> those who have work and those who don't, I say "do not let yourself be robbed of hope! Do not let yourselves be robbed of hope!" Perhaps hope is like embers under the ashes; let us help each other with solidarity, blowing on the ashes to rekindle the flame. But hope carries us onwards. That is not optimism, it is something else. However hope does not belong to any one person, we all create hope! We must sustain hope in everyone, among all of you and among all of us who are far away. Hope is both yours and ours. It is something that belongs to everyone! This is why I am saying to you: "do not let yourselves be robbed of hope!"

Then the pope extended an invitation to all the workers who were there listening: "But let us be cunning, for the Lord tells us that idols are more clever than we are. The Lord asks us to have the wisdom of serpents and the innocence of doves. Let us acquire this cunning and call things by their proper name. At this time, in our economic system, in our proposed globalized system of life there is an idol at the centre and this is unacceptable! Let us all fight so that there may be men and women, families, all of us at the centre—at least of our own life—so that hope can make headway. . . . 'Do not let yourselves be robbed of hope!'"

Francis concluded his speech spontaneously, with a prayer that came from the heart:

> Lord, you were not without a job, you were a carpenter, you were happy.
> Lord, we have no work.
> The idols want to rob us of our dignity. The unjust systems want to rob us of hope.
> Lord, do not leave us on our own. Help us to help each other; so that we forget our selfishness a little and feel in our heart the "we", the we of a people who want to keep on going.

> Lord Jesus, you were never out of work, give us work and teach
> us to fight for work and bless us all.

Francis also pronounced important words on solidarity at an
audience with the participants of an international conference
sponsored by the Centesimus Annus Pro Pontifice Foundation on
May 25, 2013.[3] "Unemployment—the lack or loss of work—is a
phenomenon that is spreading like an oil slick in vast areas of
the west and is alarmingly widening the boundaries of poverty.
Moreover there is no worse material poverty, I am keen to stress,
than the poverty which prevents people from earning their bread
and deprives them of the dignity of work."

"Well," Francis added, "'this something wrong' no longer re-
gards only the south of the world but also the entire planet. Hence
the need 'to rethink solidarity' no longer as simply assistance for
the poorest, but as a global rethinking of the whole system, as a
quest for ways to reform it and correct it in a way consistent with
the fundamental human rights of all human beings."

Francis then explained the deep meaning of solidarity: "It is
essential to restore to this word 'solidarity' viewed askance by the
world of economics—as if it were a bad word—the social citizenship
that it deserves. Solidarity is not an additional attitude, it is not a
form of social alms-giving but, rather, a social value; and it asks us
for its citizenship." Finally, going deeper into the reasons of the crisis
of recent years, Francis said, "The current crisis is not only economic
and financial but is rooted in an ethical and anthropological crisis.
Concern with the idols of power, profit, and money, rather than with
the value of the human person has become a basic norm for functioning and a crucial criterion for organization. We have forgotten
and are still forgetting that over and above business, logic and the
parameters of the market is the human being; and that something
is men and women in as much as they are human beings by virtue
of their profound dignity: to offer them the possibility of living a
dignified life and of actively participating in the common good."

We must also remember the call launched by Pope Francis from
Rio de Janeiro on the occasion of World Youth Day, which saw

the pope return to Latin America in the last week of July 2013, a few months after his election to the papacy. "I would like to make an appeal," said the pope on July 25, during the visit to the favela of Varginha, "to those in possession of greater resources, to public authorities and to all people of good will who are working for social justice: never tire of working for a more just world, marked by greater solidarity! No one can remain insensitive to the inequalities that persist in the world! Everybody, according to his or her particular opportunities and responsibilities, should be able to make a personal contribution to putting an end to so many social injustices."[4]

Therefore, "the culture of selfishness," Francis explained, "and individualism, that often prevails in our society is not, I repeat, not what builds up and leads to a more habitable world: rather, it is the culture of solidarity that does so; the culture of solidarity means seeing others not as rivals or statistics, but brothers and sisters. And we are all brothers and sisters!"

Pope Francis, citing the final document of the meeting of Latin American Bishops in Aparecida, added: "I would also like to tell you that the Church, the 'advocate of justice and defender of the poor in the face of intolerable social and economic inequalities which cry to heaven,' wishes to offer her support for every initiative that can signify genuine development for every person and for the whole person." And concluded by saying that "it is certainly necessary to give bread to the hungry—this is an act of justice. But there is also a deeper hunger, the hunger for a happiness that only God can satisfy, the hunger for dignity."

The exploitation of the poor; the unjust economic systems. Are these only problems rooted in the heart of humanity and its mismanagement of the "neutral" economic and financial means, or is there something more widespread, more extensive, more operational? In the morning homily in the Chapel of Santa Marta on May 1, 2013, the feast day of St. Joseph the Worker (and all workers), Francis referred to the social, political, and economic systems that in various places around the world are based on exploitation. Thus, they choose "not to pay what is just and strive to make maximum profit at any cost, taking advantage of others' work without worrying the least bit about their dignity. This goes against God!"[5]

Almost a year later, on March 20, 2014, at an audience with the managers and workers of the Terni steel mill, the pope said: "What can we say before the grave problem of unemployment affecting various European countries? It is the consequence of an economic system which is no longer capable of creating work, because it has placed an idol at the centre that is called money! Therefore, the various political, social and economic entities are called to promote a different approach based on justice and solidarity."[6]

chapter 4

SUCH AN ECONOMY KILLS

Christian tradition . . . has always understood this right [to private property] within the broader context of the right common to all to use the goods of the whole of creation: the right to private property is subordinated to the right to common use, *to the fact that goods are meant for everyone.*

—John Paul II, *Laborem Exercens*

Evangelii Gaudium, the apostolic exhortation dedicated to evangelization, is Pope Francis's first real programmatic document. We could also say programmatic without a real program, because Francis does not intend to "trickle down" or dictate from the top any directives of reform nor indicate specific strategies, but rather he wishes to trigger processes without controlling or defining them. It could also be considered a post-synodal apostolic exhortation, gathering the suggestions and proposals coming from the Synod on Evangelization. Francis, however, has made it a key document of his pontificate. A "road map" pointing out "new paths for the Church's journey in years to come."[1] Almost a prophecy of a profound renewal proposed to all Christians. An operational text, intended to shake up all the institutions and dynamics of the ecclesial structure, with the pressing exhortation to emancipate itself from all that encumbers the mission to proclaim the chore of the gospel message among today's men and women, as they are and not as someone would like them to be, or should be. At the heart of it all, there is the joy of the gospel.

"The joy of the gospel," as stated in the first lines of the document, "fills the hearts and lives of all who encounter Jesus. Those who accept his offer of salvation are set free from sin, sorrow, inner emptiness and loneliness. With Christ joy is constantly born anew. . . . The great danger in today's world, pervaded as it is by consumerism, is the desolation and anguish born of a complacent yet covetous heart, the feverish pursuit of frivolous pleasures, and a blunted conscience." Even many faithful, the pope observes, fall prey to this, "and end up resentful, angry and listless." Instead, "whenever we take a step towards Jesus, we come to realize that he is already there, waiting for us with open arms."

Evangelii Gaudium is not and does not want to be a document on social doctrine. The pope himself states: "This Exhortation is not a social document, and for reflection on those different themes we have a most suitable tool in the *Compendium of the Social Doctrine of the Church*, whose use and study I heartily recommend."

The short paragraphs that are dedicated to poverty, inequality, social injustice, and the idolatry of money do not therefore represent a systematic and specific treatment of the topic but fall within the broader context of a text that, once again, wants to call the church back to the heart of her mission. At several points in the exhortation, Pope Francis, reiterating what was stated by Paul VI in *Octogesima Adveniens* (1971), reminds us that the church is no longer able to say a valid and appropriate word for all the different and complex situations that arise in various parts of the world. For this reason, not only are references made to what has already been written by previous popes but also to documents of regional and national episcopal conferences from all continents, on which Francis himself draws several times, citing them "with a breadth and variety that is quite unusual," as noted by the Jesuit priest Gian Paolo Salvini in his analysis of *Evangelii Gaudium* for the Italian Jesuit journal *Civiltà Cattolica*. "The evils of our world today," continued Fr. Salvini, "are denounced with clarity, even harshly, but with the intention to better understand the context in which the church is called to evangelize today; and they are discussed in a positive and constructive manner, intended to encourage and not to rebuke, to never lose 'the joy of evangelization.'"[2] Yet, as we shall see, those few pages of the exhortation containing Francis's words on the economy have attracted much attention and also sharp criticism.

"It is not the task of the pope," writes Francis in this first apostolic exhortation of his pontificate, "to offer a detailed and complete analysis of contemporary reality, but I do exhort all the communities to an 'ever watchful scrutiny of the signs of the times.' This is in fact a grave responsibility, since certain present realities, unless effectively dealt with, are capable of setting off processes of dehumanization which would then be hard to reverse." The reference here to "all the communities" means, above all, the laity, those who do not want to give up working to change reality.

"We need to distinguish clearly," continues Francis, "what might be a fruit of the kingdom from what runs counter to God's plan. This involves not only recognizing and discerning spirits, but also—and this is decisive—choosing movements of the spirit of good and rejecting those of the spirit of evil. I take for granted the different analyses which other documents of the universal magisterium have offered, as well as those proposed by the regional and national conferences of bishops." This is another important passage: *Evangelii Gaudium* is not a document on social doctrine, but it supposes them all, and draws also on various documents proposed by the regional and national conferences of bishops, which pertain more to specific problems and circumstances of local realities.

"In this Exhortation," the pope states, "I claim only to consider briefly, and from a pastoral perspective, certain factors which can restrain or weaken the impulse of missionary renewal in the Church, either because they threaten the life and dignity of God's people or because they affect those who are directly involved in the Church's institutions and in her work of evangelization." Therefore, the document is not a systematic treatment but only makes a few references to "certain factors," which are related to the overall theme of the document—that is, evangelization.

Thus Francis describes "some challenges of today's world" and observes that "humanity is experiencing a turning-point in its history, as we can see from the advances being made in so many fields. We can only praise the steps being taken to improve people's welfare in areas such as health care, education and communications." The pope's vision is therefore realistic and does not intend to demean the progress made so far.

"At the same time we have to remember," he adds, "that the majority of our contemporaries are barely living from day to day, with dire consequences. A number of diseases are spreading. The hearts of many people are gripped by fear and desperation, even in the so-called rich countries. The joy of living frequently fades, lack of respect for others and violence are on the rise, and inequality is increasingly evident." Note here the word used by Francis, "inequality," a term that, as Fr. Salvini observed, "has a socio-economic ring to it" rather than being used with a moral connotation.[3]

"It is a struggle to live," continues the pope, "and often to live with precious little dignity. This epochal change has been set in motion by the enormous qualitative, quantitative, rapid and cumulative advances occuring in the sciences and in technology, and by their instant application in different areas of nature and of life. We are in an age of knowledge and information, which has led to new and often anonymous kinds of power."

"Just as the commandment 'Thou shalt not kill' sets a clear limit in order to safeguard the value of human life," says Francis in the most contested section of the document, "today we also have to say 'thou shalt not' to an economy of exclusion and inequality. Such an economy kills. How can it be that it is not a news item when an elderly homeless person dies of exposure, but it is news when the stock market loses two points? This is a case of exclusion. Can we continue to stand by when food is thrown away while people are starving? This is a case of inequality. Today everything comes under the laws of competition and the survival of the fittest, where the powerful feed upon the powerless. As a consequence masses of people find themselves excluded and marginalized: without work, without possibilities, without any means of escape.

"Human beings are themselves considered consumer goods to be used and then discarded. We have created a 'throw away' culture which is now spreading. It is no longer simply about exploitation and oppression, but something new. Exclusion ultimately has to do with what it means to be a part of the society in which we live; those excluded are no longer society's underside or its fringes or its disenfranchised—they are no longer even a part of it. The excluded are not the 'exploited' but the outcast, the 'leftovers.'"

Returning to a theme dear to "committed" Latin American writings, Fr. Salvini points out in his analysis of the pope's exhortation that: "The pope is no longer denouncing, as did *Rerum Novarum* during the years of Leo XIII, the exploitation of workers, but the exclusion of many individuals from active society, from work, from the future, which makes them feel useless; the pope also stresses the fact that people are being used and then thrown away, to the point of creating a 'culture of waste.'"[4]

It is also worth noting, as another Jesuit, Fr. Diego Alonso-Lasheras, pointed out in one of his comments on the few pages of the exhortation dedicated to the economy in his book *Evangelii Gaudium: il testo c'interroga* (*Evangelii Gaudium*: An Exhortation that Questions Us), that also in Spanish, the language of the original text,

> Expressions such as *No a una economía de la exclusion* or *No a un dinero que gobierna en lugar de server'* should not be interpreted as absolute rejections of the economy or money. If that were the case, the pope would have used the definite article *la* or *el,* thus conveying the idea of a more general, categorical, and absolute condemnation. The same goes for the expression *No a la nueva idolatría del dinero*, where the "idolatry of money" or of any other similar reality would be completely unacceptable for a Christian. . . . The use of the indefinite article *una* or *uno* means that there are acceptable alternatives. The pope does not reject in block the economy or money, but only a particular way of doing economy, and a particular way of using money.[5]

In the next paragraph of *Evangelii Gaudium* (no. 54), the pope makes the only explicit and "technical" example, as he mentions "trickle-down" economic theories: "In this context, some people continue to defend trickle-down theories which assume that economic growth, encouraged by a free market, will inevitably succeed in bringing about greater justice and inclusiveness in the world."

It is a theory based on the optimistic views of the economic growth of the 1950s and 1960s, according to which even the most needy layers of the population come to benefit from the fruits of such growth, thanks to market forces: a greater labor demand and an increase in productivity and wages. In short, economic growth flows automatically from the top of the social pyramid down, without the need for state intervention in favor of a more equitable income distribution. The economic strategies of the 1990s were founded specifically on this theory.

"This opinion," as Francis goes on to observe, "which has never been confirmed by the facts, expresses a crude and naïve trust in the goodness of those wielding economic power and in the sacralized workings of the prevailing economic system. Meanwhile, the excluded are still waiting. To sustain a lifestyle which excludes others, or to sustain enthusiasm for that selfish ideal, a globalization of indifference has developed." "Globalization of indifference" was the term that the pope coined during his quick visit to Lampedusa to commemorate the migrants who died at sea and to draw attention to those ongoing tragedies.

"Almost without being aware of it," writes Francis in his exhortation, "we end up being incapable of feeling compassion at the outcry of the poor, weeping for other people's pain, and feeling a need to help them, as though all this were someone else's responsibility and not our own. The culture of prosperity deadens us; we are thrilled if the market offers us something new to purchase. In the meantime all those lives stunted for lack of opportunity seem a mere spectacle; they fail to move us." The inability to cry, to be touched, to feel a wound in the flesh in the face of the tragedies of our brothers and sisters who live thousands of miles from us or before our eyes—all this defines the "globalization of indifference" that Francis condemns by calling for a reaction to this "anesthesia" of consciences.

In paragraph no. 55 of *Evangelii Gaudium*, Francis rejects the idolatry of money that characterizes our developed societies, which is a consequence of that "imperialism of money" courageously condemned eighty-two years before by Pope Pius XI in *Quadragesimo Anno*.

"One cause of this situation," observes the pope, referring to the current crisis, "is found in our relationship with money, since we calmly accept its dominion over ourselves and our societies. The current financial crisis can make us overlook the fact that it originated in a profound human crisis: the denial of the primacy of the human person! We have created new idols. The worship of the ancient golden calf (Exod 32:1-35) has returned in a new and ruthless guise in the idolatry of money and the dictatorship of an impersonal economy lacking a truly human purpose. The worldwide crisis affecting finance and the economy lays bare their imbalances and, above all, their lack of real concern for human beings; man is reduced to one of his needs alone: consumption." Therefore, we are facing not only a financial-economic crisis or a stock market crisis due to speculative investments but first and foremost a crisis of *humanity*, one dominated by consumerism and one reduced to its needs alone.

"While the earnings of a minority are growing exponentially," continues Francis, "so too is the gap separating the majority from the prosperity enjoyed by those happy few. This imbalance is the result of ideologies which defend the absolute autonomy of the marketplace and financial speculation. Consequently, they reject the right of states, charged with vigilance for the common good." Thus they call for the total freedom of markets, while any willingness on the part of nations to assume responsibility for the common good in order to protect the people "discarded" by the economy that "kills" is labeled as state control. In these few lines, Francis reminds us of the irreplaceable role of politics in the service of the common good of citizens, especially of those who are most in need. Globalization cannot prevent states, nations, or intermediary bodies from laying out a plan to build a system that, if not fair, at the very least does not increase economic inequality.

"A new tyranny," continues the pope in his analysis, "is thus born, invisible and often virtual, which unilaterally and relentlessly imposes its own laws and rules. Debt and the accumulation of interest also make it difficult for countries to realize the potential of their own economies and keep citizens from enjoying their real purchasing power. To all this we can add widespread corruption and self-serving tax evasion, which have taken on worldwide dimensions." Corruption and "self-serving tax evasion" are well-known Italian phenomena—better yet, typically Italian—where hardly a week goes by without the revelation of new corruption cases at every level and where very often our political leaders behave in the most indecorous manner possible, to say the least. It is a country where the tax burden is also higher because of its large-scale evasion.

"The thirst for power and possessions," writes Francis, "knows no limits. In this system, which tends to devour everything which stands in the way of increased profits, whatever is fragile, like the environment, is defenseless before the interests of a deified market, which becomes the only rule." Here, Francis makes an important point regarding the environment, seen as "fragile" before a "deified market."

Thus the pope disapproves of money that rules instead of serving, money that from a means becomes an end. As the old proverb goes, money is a good servant, but a bad master. "Behind this attitude," observes the pope in paragraph no. 57 of the exhortation,

> lurks a rejection of ethics and a rejection of God. Ethics has come to be viewed with a certain scornful derision. It is seen as counterproductive, too human, because it makes money and power relative. It is felt to be a threat, since it condemns the manipulation and debasement of the person. In effect, ethics leads to a God who calls for a committed response which is outside the categories of the marketplace. When these latter are abso-

lutized, God can only be seen as uncontrollable, unmanageable, even dangerous, since he calls human beings to their full realization and to freedom from all forms of enslavement. Ethics—a non-ideological ethics—would make it possible to bring about balance and a more humane social order. With this in mind, I encourage financial experts and political leaders to ponder the words of one of the sages of antiquity: "Not to share one's wealth with the poor is to steal from them and to take away their livelihood. It is not our own goods which we hold, but theirs."

The passage quoted by Francis is from one of St. John Chrysostom's sermons on Lazarus.

"A financial reform open to such ethical considerations," writes the pope, "would require a vigorous change of approach on the part of political leaders. I urge them to face this challenge with determination and an eye to the future, while not ignoring, of course, the specifics of each case. Money must serve, not rule! The Pope loves everyone, rich and poor alike, but he is obliged in the name of Christ to remind all that the rich must help, respect and promote the poor. I exhort you to generous solidarity and to the return of economics and finance to an ethical approach which favours human beings." This is a clear message to those who have political responsibilities. A call to accept less passively, almost as if they were inevitable, certain mechanisms and certain processes of the economy that "kills." It is an appeal to politicians and politics in general to recover the appropriate leadership and a clear sense of their specific mission, which is to assume responsibility for all and build a society where no one is forced to fall behind. Of course, for the pope's message and hope to become reality we would need politicians with a vision, able to trigger processes, and not just men and women concerned about their compensation or reelection and unwilling to implement positive reforms if they are not the ones to benefit directly from them at the polls. A clear example of the Italian situation is the absolute inability to implement policies in favor of families, with an adequate tax distribution based on the number of children or other dependents, and the absolute inability to come up, in a timely fashion, with research for adequate policies to encourage the rise of birthrates, as other countries have done decades ago (France, for example).

Therefore, Francis says "no to the inequality which spawns violence" and in paragraph no. 59 of *Evangelii Gaudium* he addresses the issue of security in our societies: "Today in many places we hear a call for greater security. But until exclusion and inequality in society and between peoples are reversed, it will be impossible to eliminate violence. The poor and the poorer peoples are accused of violence, yet without equal opportunities the different forms of aggression and conflict will find a fertile terrain for growth and eventually explode. When a society—whether local, national or global—is willing to leave a part of itself on the fringes, no political programmes or resources spent on law enforcement or surveillance systems can indefinitely guarantee tranquility."

"This is not the case," points out the pope, "simply because inequality provokes a violent reaction from those excluded from the system, but because the socioeconomic system is unjust at its root. Just as goodness tends to spread, the toleration of evil, which is injustice, tends to expand its baneful influence and quietly to undermine any political and social system, no matter how solid it may appear. If every action has its consequences, an evil embedded in the structures of a society has a constant potential for disintegration and death."

Evil does not only dwell in our hearts. There is also an evil "crystallized in unjust social structures," observes Francis, "which cannot be the basis of hope for a better future. We are far from the so-called 'end of history,' since the conditions for a sustainable and peaceful development have not yet been adequately articulated and realized." This is one of the strongest statements in the document, recalling one of the distortions already denounced by John Paul II in the encyclical *Sollicitudo Rei Socialis*, when the then-pope spoke of "structures of sin."

In the next paragraph of the exhortation, Pope Francis offers his reflections on consumerism:

Today's economic mechanisms promote inordinate consumption, yet it is evident that unbridled consumerism combined with inequality proves doubly damaging to the social fabric. Inequality eventually engenders a violence which recourse to arms cannot and never will be able to resolve. It serves only to offer false hopes to those clamouring for heightened security, even though nowadays we know that weapons and violence, rather than providing solutions, create new and more serious conflicts. Some simply content themselves with blaming the poor and the poorer countries themselves for their troubles; indulging in unwarranted generalizations, they claim that the solution is an "education" that would tranquilize them, making them tame and harmless. All this becomes even more exasperating for the marginalized in the light of the widespread and deeply rooted corruption found in many countries—in their governments, businesses and institutions—whatever the political ideology of their leaders.

In a following passage, Francis also reflects on urban structures and the problems of big cities, which he well knows from his years as archbishop of Buenos Aires, the Argentinian capital and megalopolis. "Cities create a sort of permanent ambivalence because, while they offer their residents countless possibilities, they also present many people with any number of obstacles to the full development of their lives." And for this reason, "Houses and neighbourhoods are more often built to isolate and protect than to connect and integrate."

At the end of this brief analysis, one neither technical nor systematic, as this was not the purpose of the document, Pope Francis cites John XXIII's famous speech at the solemn inauguration of the Second Vatican Council, when Francis's predecessor distanced himself from the "prophets of doom," explaining that "the evils of our world—and those of the Church—must not be excuses for diminishing our commitment and our fervour. Let us look upon them as challenges which can help us to grow." By forcefully condemning a sterile pessimism, observes Fr. Gian Paolo Salvini in his analysis of *Evangelii Gaudium*, "the pope wants to remind us that one of the most serious temptations that 'stifle boldness and zeal is a defeatism which turns us into querulous and disillusioned pessimists.' One of our main challenges is to show that the solution will never be to escape from a personal relationship with God, which at the same time engages us with others."[6]

Several pages later (paragraphs nos. 202–4), Francis's exhortation returns to the theme of the economy and the distribution of income: "The need to resolve the structural causes of poverty cannot be delayed," says Francis, "not only for the pragmatic reason of its urgency for the good order of society, but because society needs to be cured of a sickness which is weakening and frustrating it, and which can only lead to new crises. Welfare projects, which meet certain urgent needs, should be considered merely temporary responses. As long as the problems of the poor are not radically resolved by rejecting the absolute autonomy of markets and financial speculation and by attacking the structural causes of inequality, no solution will be found for the world's problems or, for that matter, to any problems. Inequality is the root of social ills."

We must therefore "attack" the structural causes of "inequality"; we must question the "absolute autonomy of markets and financial speculation" that for too long have been considered dogmatically unquestionable, to the point where financial perpetrators exploit the states' political decisions to their advantage.

"The dignity of each human person and the pursuit of the common good," writes Francis, "are concerns which ought to shape all economic policies. At times, however, they seem to be a mere addendum imported from without in order to fill out a political discourse lacking in perspectives or plans for true and integral development. How many words prove irksome to this system! It is irksome when the question of ethics is raised, when global solidarity is invoked, when the distribution of goods is mentioned, when reference is made to protecting labour and defending the dignity of the powerless, when allusion is made to a God who demands a commitment to justice. At other times these issues are exploited by a rhetoric which cheapens them."

Only a few days after the publication of the exhortation, Francis received immediate proof of the level of irritation caused whenever someone decides to talk about global solidarity, distribution of wealth, and controversial financial-economic systems. The pope was rudely called a Marxist with little understanding of economics—and only because he does not worship the absolute autonomy of markets. This shows that his detractors understood very clearly the message of the Argentinian pope, who in another passage of the exhortation says: "We can no longer trust in the unseen forces and the invisible hand of the market. Growth in justice requires more than economic growth, while presupposing such growth: it requires decisions, programmes, mechanisms and processes specifically geared to a better distribution of income, the creation of sources of employment and an integral promotion of the poor which goes beyond a simple welfare mentality."

In his exhortation, Francis also mentions the fundamentals of the Christian faith when facing the problems of the world, such as poverty and inequality. The gospel message is in fact characterized by a clear social content that is indisputable because "at the very heart of the Gospel is life in community and engagement with others." For Christianity the infinite dignity of each human person is therefore essential; a dignity conferred by God with the creation of man "in his image and likeness." And Jesus' redemption has a social dimension, because "God, in Christ, redeems not only the individual person, but also the social relations existing between men." Reiterating various points previously made, Francis writes: "From the heart of the Gospel we see the profound connection between evangelization and human advancement, which must necessarily find expression and develop in every work of evangelization." Human advancement is closely connected with evangelization, because to evangelize means to take care of the needs of others, to be close to others, and to share the suffering of others; it is a commitment to respect the dignity of each human person. Related to this view is the pope's insistence that the "protocol" by which Christians will be judged—as Jesus said—is to be found in chapter 25 of Matthew's gospel. Therefore, everything we do for others has a transcendental dimension: "By her very nature the Church is missionary," writes the pope, "she abounds in effective charity and a compassion which understands, assists and promotes."

But Francis clearly explains, in this regard, that the commitment for the Christian is not merely about personal gestures to the poor and those in need: it calls for a commitment that engages us at every level of our human life and being. For this reason, Francis provides the following concrete examples while speaking of the inclusion of the poor in society, peace, and social dialogue.

Regarding inclusion of the poor in society, Francis explains that to remain indifferent to the cry of the poor, to be insensitive to their needs, excludes us from God's plan. It requires a new mind-set, not just the generosity of some single random act. "We need to grow in a solidarity which 'would allow all peoples to become the artisans of their destiny,' since 'every person is called to self-fulfilment.'" Francis here is quoting Paul VI's encyclical *Populorum Progressio*. We have been entrusted with goods so that we preserve and increase them; but we do so serving the common good and giving back to the poor what they deserve.

A good example is food—specifically, how much of it is wasted in developed societies. We should all be scandalized by the fact that there is enough food for all and that hunger is caused by poor distribution and the income needed to purchase it. But we need to ensure not only food but well-being in all its aspects to make life worthwhile. Pope Francis asks for this care to become a priority, and to those who are shy and afraid of being manipulated, he says: "We should not be concerned simply about falling into doctrinal error, but about remaining faithful to this light-filled path of life and wisdom," of service to the poor. "When Saint Paul approached the apostles in Jerusalem," writes the pope, "to discern whether he was 'running or had run in vain' (Gal 2:2), the key criterion of authenticity which they presented was that he should not forget the poor (cf. Gal 2:10)." As Fr. Salvini observes in his analysis of Francis's exhortation, "It is possible that in writing this, Pope Francis was thinking of one of the cardinal electors, also from South America, who had told him immediately after he had been elected pope, 'don't forget the poor.' It is a criterion valid today, when we see growing around us a 'new self-centered paganism.'"[7]

This is also why Francis repeated in *Evangelii Gaudium* his theme that the entire journey of the Christian experience is marked by the poor: "The option for the poor is primarily a theological category rather than a cultural, sociological, political or philosophical one." And this option belongs to the most authentic tradition of the church. "This is why," he says, "I want a Church which is poor and for the poor. They have much to teach us. Not only do they share in the *sensus fidei*, but in their difficulties they know the suffering Christ."

Therefore, what Francis asks for, through the pages of *Evangelii Gaudium*, is to remove the structural causes of poverty by renouncing the absolute autonomy of markets and financial speculation. In short, we cannot let the markets govern themselves.

Francis makes clear that he is far from "proposing an irresponsible populism," and adds, "If anyone feels offended by my words, I would respond that I speak them with affection and with the best of intentions, quite apart from any personal interest or political ideology. My words are not those of a foe or an opponent." What Francis calls for is a "shared responsibility" for the good of all—that is, of the whole world. "We need a form of collaboration," says Fr. Salvini, "that safeguards the sovereignty of nations, ensures the economic well-being of all countries, and not of just a few."

"In particular, the pope would like us to be aware of the new forms of vulnerability that lead to new forms of poverty."[8]

There are plenty of examples of this vulnerability: migrants, the victims of human trafficking, the new forms of slavery and exploitation, women, unborn children, "the most defenseless and innocent among us," along with the natural environment.

In his exhortation, Francis reminds us of the duty to participate in political life, but he also states that "becoming a people demands something more" that requires an ongoing process in which "every new generation must take part." Father Salvini summarizes for us the four principles set out by the pope, and of the greatest value to him, that are "related to constant tensions present in every social reality."

These are principles that Francis believes will guide us in building peace. The first is: *"Time is greater than space,"* which means that we "need to give time to processes so that they can develop properly, without being obsessed with immediate results. In socio-political activities, it is essential to give the time necessary for processes to develop, more than possessing all the spaces of power."

The second is: *"Unity prevails over conflict."* Conflicts "are not preventable, but must be accepted, faced, and handled; they must be resolved in order to make them a link in the chain of new peace processes. 'In this way it becomes possible to build communion amid disagreement,' which does not mean erasing differences, but to resolve them on a higher plane that preserves the valuable potential of opposing positions. Christ has unified all things in himself, and the sign of this unity is peace."

The third is: *"Realities are more important than ideas."* "'Realities simply are, whereas ideas are worked out,' writes Francis in *Evangelii Gaudium*. Ideas are tools to capture, understand, and manage reality, but it is dangerous," observes Fr. Salvini in his analysis of the exhortation, "to remain in the realm of words, images, or even sophistries. The proposals of politicians often seem clear and logical, but they are rejected because those who wrote them have kept them in the realm of pure ideas reducing politics to rhetoric. It's not for nothing that Jesus, the word of God, became incarnate, became tangible reality. And this should never be lost from sight as a fundamental element of evangelization."

The fourth principle is: *"The whole is greater than the part."* There can be, and often there is, tension "between globalization and localization." But we must avoid, as Fr. Salvini explained, "getting caught up either 'in an abstract and globalized universe,' or in a 'museum of local folklore . . . doomed to doing the same things over and over, and incapable of being challenged by novelty or appreciating the beauty which God bestows beyond their borders. . . . The whole is greater than the part, but it is also greater than the sum of its parts.' We work locally, but without losing sight of the broader perspective. The vision that the pope proposes, which has already become popular, is not the sphere, 'where every point is equidistant from the centre,' but the polyhedron, 'which reflects the convergence of all its parts, each of which preserves its distinctiveness.'"[9]

chapter 5

ALLEGATIONS AGAINST A "MARXIST POPE"

In the first place, it is obvious that not only is wealth concentrated in our times but an immense power and despotic economic dictatorship is consolidated in the hands of a few, who often are not owners but only the trustees and managing directors of invested funds which they administer according to their own arbitrary will and pleasure.

—Pius XI, *Quadragesimo Anno*

Pope Francis's words stating that "while the earnings of a minority are growing exponentially, so too is the gap separating the majority from the prosperity enjoyed by those happy few" and "this imbalance is the result of ideologies which defend the absolute autonomy of the marketplace and financial speculation" have sparked many negative reactions——even among those who think of themselves as devout Catholics. "Some," noted Fr. Diego Alonso-Lasheras, "have tried to water down the words of the pope on economic issues citing the pope himself, who says that his job is not to offer a thorough analysis of contemporary reality—that is, of the economic reality. Others have tried to diminish the importance of his words by saying that it is *only* an apostolic exhortation, and therefore it is a magisterial document with less weight than that of an encyclical."[1] Among these was also Cardinal Raymond Leo Burke, who in a television interview said, referring in general terms to the content of *Evangelii Gaudium*: "It seems to me that the Holy Father made a very clear statement at the beginning that these are a number of reflections that he's making that he doesn't intend them to be part of the papal magisterium. . . . They are suggestions—he calls them guidelines. . . . I don't think it was intended to be part of the papal magisterium. At least that's my impression of it."[2] And then there were those who explicitly stated that the pope has very little understanding of economic matters.

But let us start from the most resounding attacks from the outside. Francis is a "Marxist," and the Catholic Church would be "hypocritical" if it criticizes capitalism when this is the system that finances her. This, in a nutshell, was the frantic attack launched in his typical verbal assault mode by radio commentator Rush Limbaugh against those sections of the pope's exhortation devoted to social issues. Limbaugh's words were reported all over the world, and many of course criticized his rudeness. But it would be wrong to underestimate similar attacks, because they represent the tip of the iceberg of a much broader resentment of Pope Francis coming specifically from the conservative world within the United States.

It is significant in this regard that the headline of one of Limbaugh's broadcasts was: *It's Sad How Wrong Pope Francis Is (Unless It's a Deliberate Mistranslation by Leftists)*. The pope is wrong, downright wrong in writing what he wrote, unless—this is the only justification coming from Limbaugh—what arrived in the United States was a mistranslation of the apostolic exhortation considered to be the programmatic document of Francis's pontificate. The most popular commentator of the extreme right avoided conciliatory tones: "It's sad. It's actually unbelievable. The pope has written, in part, about the utter evils of capitalism. . . . It's sad because this pope makes it very clear he doesn't know what he's talking about when it comes to capitalism and socialism and so forth." Limbaugh described *Evangelii Gaudium* as an assault on the "new tyranny of capitalism" and an attack on the "idolatry of money," and then criticized it, saying: "I have been numerous times to the Vatican. It wouldn't exist without tons of money. But regardless . . . somebody has either written this for him or gotten to him. This is just pure Marxism coming out from the mouth of the pope. Unfettered capitalism? That doesn't exist anywhere. Unfettered capitalism is a liberal socialist phrase to describe the United States. Unfettered, unregulated." After explaining the evils of socialism and the benefits of capitalism, including "trickle-down" economic policies, Limbaugh said he was "befuddled" by Francis's words: "The American Catholic Church has an annual budget of $170 billion. I think that's more than General Electric earns every year. And the Catholic Church is the largest landholder in Manhattan. I mean, they have a lot of money. They raise a lot of money. They wouldn't be able to reach out the way they do without a lot of money."[3] It is not the case here to dwell on the character and past of Francis's "accuser." But we must not forget that Limbaugh's radio talk show has about twenty million listeners, and his contract for the show is worth $400 million.

Another explicit attack directed toward Pope Francis came from Jonathan Moseley, a member of the American Tea Party movement, who in a *WorldNetDaily* article went so far as to write that "Jesus Christ is weeping in heaven hearing Christians espouse a socialist philosophy." Apparently, Jesus Christ (with whom the Tea Party is in direct communication) has rejected the theory of redistribution. Why? The answer appears to have been given by Jesus himself when asked whether it was right for a person to share an inheritance with other family members: "Jesus spoke to the individual, never to government or government policy. Jesus was a capitalist, preaching personal responsibility, not a socialist."[4]

In addition to the words of Limbaugh and Moseley, also worth mentioning are the negative comments on Francis's exhortation published by *Forbes*, the American financial magazine, according to which the pope is weighed down by his Argentine Peronist past, a search for a "third way" between capitalism and socialism, the ideas of liberation theology, and the closeness to the analysis of Nobel laureate Joseph Stiglitz.

Another famous public figure who declared himself preoccupied, better yet puzzled, by a few words written in an apostolic exhortation was the openly Catholic capitalist Kenneth Langone, cofounder of Home Depot, who owns an estimated wealth of more than $2 billion. Langone is actively involved in works of charity, supports numerous Catholic initiatives, and in 2007 was made Knight of St. Gregory the Great by Pope Benedict XVI. The Catholic magnate said he considered Francis's criticism of capitalism as "exclusionary" with regard to wealthy Catholic donors who, as a result of the pope's words, may stop funding the same Catholic Church.

We could also mention here a commentator at *Fox News* who proclaimed that "Pope Francis is the Catholic Church's Obama," or Sarah Palin's reaction, who referred to the Bishop of Rome as a "liberal," or Senator John McCain (R-AZ), who more reservedly said that he was "not particularly enamored with" Francis's economic vision. Even the Catholic congressman Peter King (R-NY) said that the pope does not understand the emancipatory aspect of the American free market economy, which in his opinion is the best economy for helping the poor raise their standard of living. While another Catholic congressman, Paul Ryan (R-WI), said that Pope Francis does not properly understand the situation: "The guy is from Argentina, they haven't had real capitalism in Argentina. They have crony capitalism in Argentina. They don't have a true free enterprise system." His argument, as we shall see in the following pages, was taken up and expanded by an authoritative exponent of American conservative Catholicism.[5]

The allegations against the "Marxist" pope thus mark the end of an era. As we shall see in a later chapter, even a few sections of Pope Benedict XVI's social encyclical *Caritas in Veritate* drew harsh criticism from American conservative circles. But it is equally true that the frantic reactions to the social message in *Evangelii Gaudium* are comparable to a sudden awakening from a dream that led some influential intellectual circles to theorize the indissoluble alliance between the church and its hierarchy, between Catholic thought and the capitalist world. An alliance that some tried to build and demonstrate through a wise and guided "pick and choose" among documents of the social doctrine of the church, selecting more "suitable" pages and lambasting others.

An alliance advocated particularly in the first decade of John Paul II's pontificate, because of the common fight against communist totalitarianism represented by the Soviet empire and its allies. The battle for religious freedom fought by John Paul II—who came from behind the Iron Curtain and supported the Polish trade union *Solidarność* (Solidarity)—and the objective convergence with some of the goals of Ronald Reagan's presidency, together with some passages of the 1991 encyclical *Centesimus Annus* in the aftermath of the collapse of the Berlin Wall and the end of the real-socialist regimes, induced some intellectuals to think (and theorize) that the Catholic Church had indissolubly married—and the doctrine of marital indissolubility is undoubtedly Catholic—a specific financial-economic system. A system that was considered not only the best (or most acceptable) of all possible worlds but also the one that, in its own way, was more "Christian," more respectful of human freedom and human initiative. In short, an arrangement that has its supporters among theorists and intellectuals who do not certainly mind that the church does charity work, and invites others to do the same, but cannot stand the possibility of someone who challenges the current configurations and systems. What's more, they also consider inappropriate even to just ask questions on certain topics, accusing those who do that they know nothing about the economy.

We also cannot fail to notice that in recent decades the most significant episcopal appointments in the United States have somehow favored candidates who more clearly adhere to this system of thought. They are less accustomed to speak out on social issues—the consequences of globalization and the financial crisis, new forms of poverty, illegal immigration, the dignity of work, and welfare—and instead focus exclusively on issues such as the fight against abortion and the opposition to the recognition of homosexual unions.

In this sense it is not wrong to think that the real point of friction after Francis's election is not so much (or not only) the pope's minor insistence on the so-called "nonnegotiable principles"—which are clearly proclaimed also in *Evangelii Gaudium*—but rather the new pope's social message and his words on poverty. A message that, despite being clearly in line with the teachings of the social doctrine of the church, resonate more powerfully not because of its content but because of the amnesia in which that same content has fallen in recent years (at least in some Catholic circles).

There is the feeling, in fact, that even Pius XI's eloquent and prophetic words in *Quadragesimo Anno*, written more than eighty years ago, in the aftermath of the Wall Street crash of 1929, but still applicable following the recent economic and financial crisis, are considered too extreme or radical even within certain Vatican spheres. It is not uncommon, in fact, to encounter there some discomfort for the insistence on social issues, which until now has been justified on two grounds. First, there is the risk of ideology—that is, the manipulation of faith for political purposes—as in certain currents of liberation theology. Second, priority must be given to evangelization—that is, the proclamation of the gospel today, which should be the main focus of the church and its representatives—as if evangelization has nothing to do with men and women's living conditions and, therefore, with the commitment to human advancement as its immediate goal. But insisting on justifying this generalized discomfort in speaking of the poor, of poverty, of "unequal" economic systems, ends up obscuring not just some sections but entire pages of Catholic social teaching.

We mentioned at the beginning of this chapter some of the more vehement and direct attacks against Pope Francis's exhortation coming from the United States. A few weeks after the publication of *Evangelii Gaudium*, a more cautious, articulate, and reasoned criticism has come from the pen of Michael Novak, author of *The Spirit of Democratic Capitalism,* in which he sanctified the union between Catholics and Republicans in that religious, but also political, alliance sponsored in the 1980s by President Ronald Reagan against world communism.[6] In an article published in the conservative weekly *National Review,* Novak writes:

"Reading the new exhortation by Pope Francis after the wildly misleading presentations of it by the *Guardian* and Reuters (both from the left side of the U.K. press), and reading it with an American ear for language, I was at first amazed at how partisan and empirically unfounded were five or six of its sentences."

"But reading the exhortation in full in its English translation, and reading it through the eyes of a professor-bishop-pope who grew up in Argentina, I began to have more sympathy for the phrases used by Pope Francis."[7]

Novak recalled having had the opportunity to study the early writings of John Paul II: "From 1940 (under the Nazi/Soviet occupation) until 1978 (when he moved to the Vatican), Karol Wojtyla had virtually no experience of a capitalist economy and a democratic/republican polity. To come to understand the concepts behind that sort of political economy, he had to listen closely and learn a quite different vocabulary."

Novak's words suggest a conviction that Francis, as John Paul II did before him, will eventually learn how to speak properly of "capitalist economy." Novak, recalling that he had lectured "in Argentina and in Chile since the late 1970s," said that he read "the entire exhortation with an ear for echoes of daily economic and political life in Argentina."

"In my visits to Argentina," continued Novak, "I observed a far sharper divide between the upper middle class and the poor than any I had experienced in America. In Argentina I saw very few paths by which the poor could rise out of poverty. In the U.S., many of those who are now rich or middle class had come to America (or their parents had) dirt poor, many of us not speaking English, with minimal schooling, and with mainly menial skills. But before us lay many paths upward. As Peru's Hernando de Soto stresses, the U.S. had the rule of law and clear property rights, on which one could safely build over generations."

"Virtually all my acquaintances while I was growing up had experienced early poverty. Our grandfathers," wrote Novak, "were garment workers, steelworkers, store clerks, gardeners, handy-men, blue-collar workers of all sorts, without social insurance, Medicaid, food stamps, housing allowances, or the like. But they labored and somehow were able to send their children to colleges and universities. Now their children are doctors, lawyers, professors, editors, and owners of small businesses all over the country."

Novak then explained that in his *Inquiry into the Nature and Causes of the Wealth of Nations* (1776), Adam Smith compared the economic history of Latin America with that of North America and "noted that in Latin America there were still many institutions of feudal Europe—large landholders, plantations, plantation workers. In North America, only the southern United States was something like that. Throughout Latin America, for almost two centuries at the time Smith wrote, many economic powers and permissions were doled out by government officials in far-off Spain or Portugal."

"Besides, experience in the Anglosphere had led to a distrust of monarchs and their courts, and later of barons and dukes and the aristocracy as a whole, since these people could not be counted on either to see or to serve the common good. By contrast, the opposite habit of mind had grown throughout the Latin world. There, officials of the state were regularly entrusted," observed Novak, "with minding the common good, despite a long record of official betrayals of duty, outbreaks of tyranny, and the use of economic resources to enrich successive leaders of the state. In Latin America, the pluralistic private sector was mistrusted, but not the state."

Novak's article continues with a presentation of what happened in the United States, where "under a government strictly limited by law, there grew up almost universal property ownership by individuals (except under the evil institution of slavery, America's primal sin), a large swath of small enterprises, and a huge base of prospering small farms. Smith described the creation of wealth in North America as welling up from below, from the prosperity at the bottom, where frugal habits led to wise investments in railroads, canals, and other large business corporations."

According to Novak, John Paul II

> recognized this huge social change in *Centesimus Annus* (*The Hundredth Year*, 1991), of which paragraph 32 opens: "In our time, in particular, there exists another form of ownership which is no less important than land: *the possession of know-how, knowledge, and skill.* The wealth of the industrialized nations is based much more on this kind of ownership than on natural resources." The rest of this paragraph is concise in its penetration of the

causes of wealth and the role of human persons and associations in the virtue of worldwide solidarity, of which globalization is the outward expression.

Pope John Paul II quickly recognized that today "the decisive factor [in production] is increasingly *man himself*, that is, his knowledge, especially his scientific knowledge, his capacity for interrelated and compact organization, as well as his ability to perceive the needs of others and to satisfy them."

Novak then cited paragraph no. 42 of the same encyclical, in which John Paul II "defined his ideal capitalism, succinctly, as that economic system springing from creativity, under the rule of law, and 'the core of which is ethical and religious.' In his first social encyclical ten years earlier, *Laborem Exercens* (*On Human Work*, 1981), directly rejecting orthodox Marxist language about labor, the pope had already begun to project 'creation theology' as a replacement for 'liberation theology.'"

In the following years—according to Novak—John Paul II addressed the concept of human capital. "Step by step, he thought his way to his own vision of the economy best suited to the human person—not perfectly so, in this vale of tears, but better than any rival, Communist or traditional. John Paul II set it forth as 'the model which ought to be proposed to the countries of the Third World which are searching for the path to true economic and civil progress.'"

Let us not lose track of the path delineated so far by Novak, an advocate of the "holy alliance" between Catholicism and capitalism. According to him, the church, with John Paul II's pontificate, has taken the path of rapprochement. And to validate this there are concrete historical reasons.

"As the 20th century began," wrote Novak, "Argentina was ranked among the top 15 industrial nations, and more and more of its wealth was springing from modern inventions rather than farmland. Then a destructive form of political economy, just then spreading like a disease from Europe—a populist fascism with tight government control over the economy—dramatically slowed Argentina's economic and political progress. Instability in the rule of law undermined economic creativity. Inflation blew to impossible heights. (I brought home from Argentina in the early 1980s a note for a million Argentine pesos that had declined in worth to two American pennies.)"

"Over three generations," added Novak, "very little of the nation's natural wealth and opportunity for social advancement has overflowed into the upraised buckets of the poor. Upward mobility from the bottom up was (and is) infrequent. Today, the lot of Argentina's poor is still static. The poor receive little personal instruction in turning to independent creativity and initiative. . . . Human energies are drained by dependency on state benefits. The visible result has been a largely static society, with little opportunity for the poor to rise out of poverty."

According to Novak, if Pope Francis in *Evangelii Gaudium* refers to this situation, his analysis is actually accurate. In many Latin American countries, "today's corporate leaders are often the grandsons of the great landholders of the past. Some of these are men of vision, invention, and personal initiative who have built their own firms. Yet as of now most Americans cannot name a single household item invented by a Latin American."

To put it bluntly, Novak's point here is that Pope Francis may be right, as long as we confine his words to the situation in Argentina or, at most, Latin America. But if we shift them to a global context and apply them to the United States—always the real point of contention—then the pope is wrong.

Novak believes that some of the "swipes are so highly partisan and biased that they seem outside this pope's normal tranquillity and generosity of spirit. Exactly these partisan phrases were naturally leapt upon by media outlets such as Reuters and the *Guardian*. Among these are 'trickle-down theories,' 'invisible hand,' 'idolatry of money,' 'inequality,' and trust in the state 'charged with vigilance for the common good.'"

Citing "one of the shrewdest observers of Latin America today," Mary Anastasia O'Grady, Novak asks, "Why is it then . . . 'that most of today's desperate poor are concentrated in places where the state has gained an outsize role in the economy specifically on just such grounds'? Ever since Max Weber, Catholic social thought has been blamed for much of the poverty in many Catholic nations. Pope Francis inadvertently adds evidence for Weber's thesis."

Novak considers it desirable that some economic historian set "each of these highly inflammable and partisan charges in context," to explain "what each meant to the author who originated them, as opposed to the partisan usage of today's media." In the rest of his long article, Novak deals with the pope's words on "trickle-down" theories, contesting the English rendering of the Spanish *derrame* with "trickle-down": "the English translation introduces both a sharply different meaning and a harsh new tone into this passage. Only those hostile to capitalism and Reagan's successful reforms, and to the policies of Republicans in general after the downward mobility of the Carter years, use the derisive expression 'trickle-down,' intended to caricature what actually happened under Reagan, namely, dramatic upward mobility."

The observation in *Evangelii Gaudium* according to which the positive aspects of "trickle-down" theories have never been confirmed by the facts is understandable "in Argentina and other static systems with no upward mobility," but in nations like the United States, with "generations of reliable upward mobility, it is not true at all. . . . Despite its glaring faults, especially in its entertainment sector—obscene and sexually explicit pop music, decadent images and themes in movies—the American system has been more 'inclusive' of the poor than any other nation on earth."

Novak concludes that he appreciates two aspects of the exhortation: the affirmation that "the entire cosmos, and the whole of human life, are upward-leaping flames from the inner life of the Creator, from *caritas*—that outward-moving creative love that is God"—and the focus of *Evangelii Gaudium* on "the main practical task of our generation: breaking the last round of chains of ancient poverty."

Of course, Novak reiterates that "whatever one prays in worship on Sunday gets its truthfulness from what Christians actually do in their daily lives to help the poor. If one doesn't come to the aid of the poor, one does not love God." *Evangelii Gaudium* therefore does not claim to be "a teaching document laying out a careful argument—that is the task for an encyclical. Rather, it is more like a sermon, a somewhat informal occasion for the pope to set out his vision as a pastor." While in the future, Novak adds with a hope, Pope Francis "will unfold his fuller arguments about the political economy that best helps the poor to move out of poverty. I can only imagine that consultations on the subject have already begun. I hope the pope's aides will begin with the experience-impelled conclusion, a bit reluctantly advanced, in the well-reasoned pathway of paragraph 42 of John Paul II's *Centesimus Annus*."

Notice here two specific statements. First, the downgrading of the papal document to a simple "homily" and, second, the hope that Francis will follow in John Paul II's footsteps and that before writing other documents on social and economic issues he will be assisted by his "aides," along the lines of certain U.S. circles and think tanks.

The dogma that Novak has been theorizing and arguing for so far is simple: let the church go on speaking about the poor and charity; let her remind us that we ought to give alms; let her offer us ethical guidance; let her fight her battles in defense of life and against the deterioration of certain customs in our decadent Western societies; let her remind us that we must strive to be good and honest. But may she never dare to ask one single question on the current system of capitalism—that same system that at present has no more contact with the real economy and is dominated by the financial markets.

To quote Pius XI's words (another pope who evidently had no adequate "aides") in the encyclical *Quadragesimo Anno* at paragraph no. 109:

> The ultimate consequences of the individualist spirit in economic life are those which you yourselves, Venerable Brethren and Beloved Children, see and deplore: Free competition has destroyed itself; economic dictatorship has supplanted the free market; unbridled ambition for power has likewise succeeded greed for gain; all economic life has become tragically hard, inexorable,

and cruel. To these are to be added the grave evils that have resulted from an intermingling and shameful confusion of the functions and duties of public authority with those of the economic sphere—such as, one of the worst, the virtual degradation of the majesty of the State, which although it ought to sit on high like a queen and supreme arbitress, free from all partiality and intent upon the one common good and justice, is become a slave, surrendered and delivered to the passions and greed of men. And as to international relations, two different streams have issued from the one fountain-head: On the one hand, economic nationalism or even economic imperialism; on the other, a no less deadly and accursed internationalism of finance or international imperialism whose country is where profit is.

These words were written in 1931, but they are still extremely valid today—better yet, *especially* today. Thus, is there the possibility for us to question—not to eliminate, but to try to change—the system? "When I give food to the poor," said Hélder Câmara, bishop of Recife, "they call me a saint. When I ask why the poor have no food, they call me a communist." The pope has been called a "Marxist," or to put it more mildly, they say that he knows nothing of economics.

"Novak's resentment," says the philosopher Max Borghesi in an article published on the website *Il Sussidiario*, "is understandable. Exalted as the 'Catholic' Max Weber, who instead of Weber's *The Protestant Ethic and the Spirit of Capitalism* has placed 'Catholic' ethic as the true foundation of 'democratic' capitalism, now finds himself with a pontificate that has no faith in that system that he, for quite some time now, helped legitimize and raise above any possible accusation."[8]

According to Borghesi, Novak did not like "especially the idea that the capitalist model has not been confirmed by the facts as a source of general well-being." Novak's criticism, wrote Borghesi,

> demonstrates, in its edginess, that *Evangelii Gaudium* has hit the mark. . . . After 1989, as we have grown accustomed to the legitimization, with no ifs and buts, of capitalist globalization, celebrated as the "end of history" and as a panacea for all evils,

any criticism to this system is perceived as being tainted with crypto-communism. *Evangelii Gaudium* breaks through this wall of silence, and is like a formidable pebble thrown into a still pond of ideas. Benedict XVI had already given it a shot, with his *Caritas in Veritate*, an encyclical that contained important points, and good critical insights. If we compare the two, Francis' apostolic exhortation appears more resolute; it takes the bull by the horns, and is not afraid to proclaim to the world the limits, obvious to everyone after the 2008 financial debacle, of an economic model that, left to itself, is likely to overwhelm the world.

"How many words prove irksome to this system! . . . We can no longer trust in the unseen forces and the invisible hand of the market," wrote Francis in *Evangelii Gaudium*. The economic bodies cannot claim absolute autonomy, or, even less, have priority over politics, which instead appears today, as we shall see, almost at the service of the financial markets. We need therefore a return to the primacy of politics, inasmuch as it has the common good at heart.

"One thing is certain:" observes Borghesi, "rarely has a text of the social teaching of the Church spoken more forcefully. What strikes, in Francis' exhortation, is the tone, the shift from the descriptive mode to the first person, the pope's direct involvement, the indignation in the face of a world that would have all the possible means to alleviate the suffering and marginalization of millions of human beings and yet does nothing. 'The Pope loves everyone, rich and poor alike, but he is obliged in the name of Christ to remind all that the rich must help, respect and promote the poor.' A provocation that, apparently, neither *Forbes* magazine, nor Michael Novak, liked much."

Although *Evangelii Gaudium* focused on evangelization and social issues, it drew criticisms from the world of investment banks as well. On December 2, 2013, JP Morgan Chase economist Jim Glassman, without ever naming the pope, defended market economies and their "effectiveness" in saving people from poverty: "Those concerned about global poverty," wrote Glassman, "have more to be thankful for today than to complain about. The commonly-heard complaints that today's economic systems fail to address the plight of the poor ignore several fundamental facts."[9]

Glassman then added in his research note that "poverty is not a modern phenomenon." Then he went on to explain that "the developed economies are still recovering from deep recessions and in time will reach their full potential. That is, of course, why central bank policies remain so stimulative. Those hurt by the recession will be restored as the developed economies continue to recover." (This is not, however—regardless whether one is religious or not—the true picture of what we are facing.)

The third point in his memorandum is that "despite the cyclical problems of the developed economies, the average global living standard is at a record high. . . . In other words, market-oriented economic systems are doing more to cure global poverty than any other effort in the past." Thus, according to Glassman, the current market-oriented economic system works and helps; it is doing very much indeed. We must trust in it and not complain, or make ill-chosen questions. We must believe in its dogma.

Another similar critique of the pope's words came on December 23, 2013, from John Gapper, a well-known columnist for the *Financial Times*, who, commenting on the exhortation, said that Francis is "wrong" on the issue of global inequality. The commentator of the authoritative newspaper on economic and financial issues took aim at paragraph no. 56 of *Evangelii Gaudium* against ideologies that defend the absolute autonomy of the markets and financial speculation. "His words resonated with many people who face the seemingly inexorable rise of the richest 1 percent," wrote Gapper, who admitted that the gap between rich and poor has grown in the West, but in recent years economic inequality has declined globally. Citing the Gini Index on global inequality, the *Financial Times* columnist noted that in China, India, Brazil, and other emerging countries where the vast majority of the world population lives, inequality has declined due to "global capitalism."[10]

"Not only has income distribution become more equal," said Gapper, "but capitalism can take the credit." *Evangelii Gaudium* is merely the expression of the discontent of "the Western middle class" affected by the financial crisis and the recession.

According to Gapper, the 2008–9 financial crisis was only a glitch, an unpredictable factor. There is no need to change the model, the system, or better yet, the dogma.

Alessandro Corneli, in an article in *Global Research & Report Group*, observed that the *Financial Times*, by juxtaposing the data on global poverty while highlighting progress in emerging countries, is avoiding an "answer [to] the real question raised by the pope: the philosophy behind this economic mechanism that increases the gap between the richest and the poorest, as recently admitted by President Barack Obama himself, who pointed out that while in the past top managers received an income of 20 to 30 times higher than that of an average worker now it is 273 times higher."[11]

The criticism expressed by certain capitalist circles have found within the church no lack of support. Cardinal Franc Rodé, former prefect of the Congregation for Religious, gave an interview in September 2013 to the Slovenian national press agency, criticizing Pope Francis. For the Slovenian cardinal the pope is "too much of the left." "No doubt," said Rodé, "the pope is a genius of communication. He communicates very well with the crowd, the media, and the faithful. . . . A great advantage is that he seems likable. On the other hand, his opinions, on capitalism and social justice, are excessively to the left. One sees how he is shaped by the environment from which he comes. In South America, there are enormous social differences, and great debates on this situation emerge every day. But those people talk too much, and solve few problems."[12]

Rodé, who lived for many years in Argentina at the time when Slovenia was part of communist Yugoslavia, as archbishop of Ljubljana led the Slovenian church toward a strong capitalist model—a model, however, that has had disastrous results. For instance, the Slovenian Diocese of Maribor suffered a financial crisis due to bad investments, which included financial holdings and embarrassing financial links to a television network that at some point even aired pornography. Already at the time of Pope Benedict XVI the Holy See was forced to intervene.

In order to understand how certain circles are irritated by the church's increased attention to social issues, the case of Francis's appointment of the new archbishop of Chicago is particularly enlightening. On September 20, 2014, the successor to Cardinal Francis George was announced; the new bishop at the helm of the Archdiocese of Chicago is Blase Joseph Cupich. Born in 1949, and bishop since 1998, first in Rapid City, South Dakota, and then Spokane, Washington, Cupich was not even considered among the initial favorites for the position.

In the preceding months, however, it was precisely Cupich who embraced the words of the apostolic nuncio concerning Francis's instructions for the American church: "Pope Francis doesn't want cultural warriors; he doesn't want ideologues."[13] In 2011, Cupich encouraged his priests and seminarians to refrain from organizing and participating in sit-in prayers at abortion clinics. He recalled the political polarization on this issue by noting that decisions on abortion are not usually taken outside clinics but "around kitchen tables and in living rooms and they frequently involve a sister, daughter, relative or friend who may have been pressured or abandoned by the man who fathered the child."[14] Therefore, priests needed to intervene in *those* moments and not later.

In April 2012, the American press noticed the restraint with which Cupich had reacted to Obama's health care reform; he confirmed the opinion shared by the episcopate on certain issues, but not as vehemently as his fellow bishops. So rare was this in the ecclesial landscape and American media that it became immediately newsworthy. In a post on his blog, Bryan Cones, editor of *US Catholic* defined Cupich as "the bishop who can speak without shouting."[15] Such an approach can, according to Cupich himself, "really produce something in the long run," whereas the caustic jokes and belligerent style soon run out of steam.[16]

Cupich had also defended the more social sections of *Evangelii Gaudium* from criticism of the ultra-libertarian American conservatives, reminding them of the value of solidarity between peoples and denouncing their positions as inconsistent with the social doctrine of the church. We should not forget that when

Cupich was bishop of Rapid City the diocesan "Pro-Life Committee" became the "Social Justice Committee." Anti-abortion messages did not cease to circulate, but the spectrum of the operations broadened, as the committee began targeting the death penalty, immigration reform, and poverty.

In a letter written from Rome after the appointment of Cupich, Kishore Jayabalan, director of the Acton Institute (a Catholic think tank whose mission is to disseminate the principles of a free society and free-market system) in the Italian capital, revealed his discontent for the change of course evident in the appointment of the new bishop.

"With the recent nomination of Bishop Blase Cupich as the next Archbishop of Chicago, we are likely entering the latest round of polemics over the purported incompatibility of Catholicism and capitalism, Windy-City style. In honor of Sean Connery, we'll be sure not to bring a knife to this gun fight."[17]

One of the reasons that induced Jayabalan to write his letter was "Bishop Cupich's participation at a June 2014 conference at the Catholic University of America in Washington, DC. The title of that conference, *Erroneous Autonomy: The Catholic Case Against Libertarianism*, tells you all you need to know about its conclusions. The videos don't reveal how many people took part, but it took place around the same time as Acton University, where we had nearly 1,000 people from all over the world trying to bring markets and morality together in a constructive fashion."

A second reason for concern, according to Jayabalan, was "the portrayal of Cupich as a new kind of leader—a 'Francis Bishop'—who eschews the culture wars over abortion, same-sex marriage, and other contentious issues—all having to do with the Church's teachings on sexuality—and focuses on supposedly non-controversial matters like immigration and youth unemployment because 'this economy kills.' (Cue Rodney King in the pulpit.) Many on the religious left are hoping for the demise of nasty ideologues like Paul Ryan and the Acton Institute who have the gall to promote economic liberty as a path to material and perhaps spiritual well-being, and may even commit the mortal sin of voting Republican."

Notice here the clear reference to *Evangelii Gaudium* and the expression "religious left." Apparently, for these think tanks the mere allusion to issues such as poverty and social justice in terms that do not exalt the progressive and happy destiny of capitalism is reason enough to cause alarm.

"This recurring animus against free markets" continued Jayabalan, "may come as a surprise to those of us who have, and especially to those who haven't, enjoyed the benefits of freedom, innovation and wealth creation. Didn't we put the mythology of 'real socialism' to rest with Pope St. John Paul II's 1991 encyclical *Centesimus Annus*? John Paul certainly didn't idolize the market economy and warned that it will succeed only to the degree that it respects moral and ethical principles that come from outside the field of economics. The world's financial and business scandals continually remind us of this truth. At some point, however, we have to regard this hostility to markets as the ideological equivalent as that some libertarians have towards the State."

Jayabalan did admit that Cupich's positions are more nuanced than those of Óscar Rodríguez Maradiaga, archbishop of Tegucigalpa, Honduras, and president of Caritas Internationalis, evidently considered by Jayabalan as lost to the faith in capitalism and its indisputable dogmas.

"To be fair," wrote Jayabalan,

> Bishop Cupich's reading of libertarianism was not nearly as extreme as Óscar Rodríguez Maradiaga's account. I've heard the latter give similar talks in person on several occasions and his views never seem to change, no matter what evidence exists to the contrary. His Eminence has no patience for reforming or improving "the idol" of market economies; he wants to smash and replace it with nothing but love (try paying your bills with that!), where Cupich asserts that libertarians simply don't believe in solidarity and apply economics to every aspect of life. Cupich, of course, is American and Rodriguez is from Honduras, so the differences in perceptions and realities between North and South America are definitely major factors in how one appraises capitalism. But I think there's more to these kinds of remarks than geography or even culture.

According to Jayabalan,

> It has something to do with accepting the idea that economic thinking inevitably becomes the only way of looking at the world and crowds out everything else; it's a new form of the materialist determinism expounded by Marx and his followers. While religious critics of capitalism often fashion themselves as simple pastors and allies of the downtrodden, "men very often find themselves in a sad state because they do not give enough thought and consideration to these things," as Pope Paul VI put it in his encyclical on development (*Populorum Progressio*, no. 85). The problem is the denial to see economics for what it is, or at least what it used to be before the mathematicians took over, i.e. a fundamentally *human* science.

"I don't expect bishops to have PhDs in economics," continued Jayabalan, "but some appreciation of the new opportunities provided by free markets would be very much welcomed by those of us who want to see growing economies lift people out of poverty. Would it be so bad to hear a bishop say that onerous levels of taxes and regulations make poverty more, rather than less, likely? Would it be impossible for a bishop to say that the freedom to buy and sell licit goods and services doesn't mean we have the freedom to beat our wives or exploit each other sexually? Would it be that hard to convince their flock that they can run successful businesses without endangering their eternal souls?"

Jayabalan is here reproposing, as we shall see, the paradigm that tends to blame the states' control and interventions, the welfare system, and taxes for all our financial problems—problems that no doubt would be solved if only there was more freedom within the marketplace.

As we might expect from such a conservative critique, the bishops are the ones who speak of these issues without fully understanding them, or understanding too little. Apparently, they need an education first. "In order to be truly effective pastors," judged Jayabalan, "bishops need to be more than 'pastoral' in the simple-minded sense of the word. As a highly-educated segment of the Church and the population in general, they have the responsibility of understanding the intellectual challenges presented by modern society, where authority, tradition and order have much less appeal than concepts such as liberty and equality. The alternative is to allow even more radical notions of autonomy to take root, placing the Church at an even greater disadvantage. Unfortunately, these intellectual challenges require thinking more seriously about mundane activities like commerce than most theologians and philosophers would like to do."

"Thanks be to God," concluded Jayabalan,

> the survival of the Church does not depend on its intellectual sophistication, so I have no doubt the Church will survive this latest bout of misinformed economics and overheated rhetoric among its leaders. As an Acton colleague of mine puts it, personal sanctity is the most important thing and some of our bishops will probably be assigned to the "bad economics" part of heaven. That would be ok if so many others didn't have to suffer the consequences of bad economics (poverty, stagnation, wasted resources, increased frustration and envy, and yes, even youth unemployment) in the meantime. Let's assume that religious leaders are acting out of sincere concern for the poor. So why do bishops hold views that manifestly hurt those they are trying to help? Perhaps, as the French poet Charles Péguy once remarked, "It will never be known what acts of cowardice have been motivated by the fear of looking insufficiently progressive."

No doubt about it; it was enough for Cupich to participate in an event during which the absolute autonomy of the markets was discussed, along with his defense of the more social sections of *Evangelii Gaudium*, to deserve this sarcastic reaction. Alas, this poor pope and his poor bishops speak of poverty and capitalism, social justice, and the idolatry of money without knowing what they are talking about. They should study economics; they should be advised by experts. Only then will they understand that they should be dealing with only certain issues, such as the fight against gay marriage. Know your place; don't step out of line, dusting off old and obsolete concepts of the social doctrine of the church that seem imbued with socialist theories.

To conclude, it is worth citing also the response that Cardinal Francis George, archbishop emeritus of Chicago and Cupich's predecessor, gave during an interview on Francis's social teaching, pointing out the extent to which the new pope's concerns are "only" for the poor.

"There is a gap between any Pope and those who would accept our economic system uncritically. The major criticisms of any economic theory are in Catholic Social Teaching: the universal destination of all material goods, the treatment of the poor as the gauge of a just economic system, the need for some regulation of markets so that return on capital does not completely outrun gains from wages, the social mortgage of private property, etc."[18]

"Both Pope John Paul II and Pope Benedict," continued Cardinal George, "contributed to rather sophisticated advances in the church's teaching on economic order. They were able to address the technical challenges of supply-side economics, the production of wealth so that more wealth can be distributed, the creation of an economic order founded on 'gift.' Pope Francis, so far, with the poor uniquely at the center of his concerns, has focused on distribution. This is a common criticism of religious leaders: they understand distribution but not production. As challenges to an economic system that is still far from what the Gospel would encourage us to work for, Pope Francis' statements ring true; as judgments on economic theory as such, a lot more has to be said."

"The Pope speaks, it seems, from the experience and the analysis of South Americans," added the cardinal, "who believe that some are rich because others are deliberately kept poor, that the 'system of neo-liberalism' captures capitalism in its entirety. It remains true that no Catholic can view the operation of our economy uncritically."

Notice here how the cardinal rephrases, albeit with cautious and respectful words, the same cliché of the pope who speaks from his experience as a "South American"—the same cliché used by certain ecclesial circles and the U.S. media, as in Europe and Italy, as a way to belittle the pope's message.

chapter 6

A FINANCE THAT FEEDS ON ITSELF

*The easy gains that a market unrestricted by any law opens to
everybody attracts large numbers to buying and selling goods,
and they, their one aim being to make quick profits with the least
expenditure of work, raise or lower prices by their uncontrolled
business dealings so rapidly according to their own caprice and
greed that they nullify the wisest forecasts of producers.*

—Pius XI, *Quadragesimo Anno*

Could it be that the pope and, more generally, the social doctrine
of the church are wrong? Is it correct to say that the concerns
expressed in *Evangelii Gaudium* are disproportionate, or do not
reflect reality? Do we really need good economic advisers to draft
encyclicals, to make them appear less in conflict with certain
forms of capitalism?

"It wouldn't be that easy," said Jesuit Fr. Diego Alonso-Lasheras,
"to say to the relatives of the more than 1,138 people who died
in the Rana Plaza in Dhaka, Bangladesh, on April 24, 2013, that
certain ways of doing economics do not kill."[1] The building on
the outskirts of the capital of Bangladesh contained hundreds of
microtextile companies, for which thousands of workers were
working for starvation wages on behalf of major international
brands. Almost two years since that tragedy the victims' families
are still waiting for adequate compensation. It is also difficult
not to admit that the majority of the world population lives in
unacceptable conditions and is excluded from economic cycles.

On October 28, 2014, a UNICEF report titled *Children of the Recession* was made public. It attests to the existence of more than 76 million children who live in poverty in rich countries—an increase shown in 23 of the 41 countries of the Organisation for Economic Co-operation and Development (OECD).[2] In the United States child poverty has grown more extreme during this recession than in that of 1982, according to UNICEF, and measures put in place to alleviate such poverty have not been so effective for the jobless poor. Since the crisis, as shown in the report, "child poverty has increased in 34 of the 50 states." According to UNICEF's head of global policy and strategy, Jeffrey O'Malley, it is a "great leap backwards" for many rich countries with "long-lasting repercussions" for children and their communities.[3]

It is also difficult not to recognize the many cases of people who have fallen victim to the "idolatry of money," at the expense of the suffering of many. That the financial crisis has a moral dimension is not an idea original to the pope but is also endorsed by those who deal with economy, as evidenced by a research from the Max Planck Sciences Po Center on Coping with Instability in Market Societies, titled *Moral Categories in the International Financial Crisis*.[4] Obviously, this does not mean that all those who have responsibility in the economic field are corrupt, but "certainly," as Fr. Alonso-Lasheras observed, "you may find among them examples that demonstrate the inequalities denounced by the pope."[5]

In 2011, the Pontifical Council for Justice and Peace published *Towards Reforming the International Financial and Monetary Systems in the Context of Global Public Authority*. The document recalled how in its 2007 annual report the International Monetary Fund had recognized, on the one hand, the close connection between a process of globalization not properly ruled and, on the other, the huge inequalities in the world. The Pontifical Council recognized that the process of globalization "with its positive aspects is at the root of the great development of the world economy in the twentieth century." Between 1900 and 2000 the world's population has almost quadrupled, and the growth in wealth produced in the world has grown much faster, resulting in a sharp increase of average per capita income. At the same time, however, the distribution of wealth did not become fairer but in many cases has worsened.

As the document states, to drive the world in this "problematic direction for its economy and also for peace" has been "an economic liberalism that spurns rules and controls."[6]

"Economic liberalism," as the document explains, "is a theoretical system of thought, a form of 'economic *apriorism*.' It purports to derive the laws for how markets function from theory, these being laws of capitalistic development, but it exaggerates certain aspects of markets and downplays or ignores others. An economic system of thought that sets down a priori the laws of market functioning and economic development, without measuring them against reality, risks becoming a tool subordinated to the interests of the countries that effectively enjoy a position of economic and financial advantage. . . ."

"The inequalities and distortions of capitalist development," according to the document, are not only the result "of economic liberalism but also of utilitarian thinking: that is, theoretical and practical approaches according to which *what is useful for the individual leads to the good of the community*." In the 1920s, some economists had already warned "about giving too much weight, in the absence of regulations and controls, to theories which have since become prevailing ideologies and practices on the international level."

A "devastating effect of these ideologies" is the crisis in which the world finds itself still immersed.

Are these excessive worries? Unproven theories? Neoliberal theories argue that markets, if left free to act, are naturally effective and equipped with self-regulating mechanisms. According to this way of thinking, the government action to help either demand or production distorts the self-regulating mechanism of the market and creates problems. The thesis that the blame for the crisis can be attributed not to the speculative market, but to the old forms of statism, emerges quite clearly also as judgment on the economic and financial crisis that began in 2008. Illuminating in this regard is the document published by the European research sector of JP Morgan Chase in June 2013: "In the early days of the crisis, it was thought that these national legacy problems were largely economic: over-levered sovereigns, banks and households, internal real exchange rate misalignments, and structural rigidities. But, over time it has become clear that there are also national legacy problems of a political nature. The constitutions and political settlements in [Europe's] southern periphery, put in place in the aftermath of the fall of fascism, have a number of features which appear to be unsuited to further integration in the region." These constitutions "tend to show a strong socialist influence, reflecting the political strength that left wing parties gained after the defeat of fascism."[7]

Therefore, "political systems around the periphery typically display several of the following features: weak executives; weak central states relative to regions; constitutional protection of labor rights; consensus building systems which foster political clientalism; and the right to protest if unwelcome changes are made to the political status quo. The shortcomings of this political legacy have been revealed by the crisis."

Without wanting to defend the indefensible of our political leaders, it is really surprising that those financial markets that contributed to the crisis and continue to fuel the speculative bubble complain because our constitutions protect workers by giving them the right to protest. According to certain financial circles, of which JP Morgan is an expression, in order to get out of the crisis we should reduce states' public spending, cut the welfare, and maybe take away workers' rights. But is it really so? Is this really the right recipe? Why do we not ask instead how it was and is possible for the financial markets to fool the economy, sending "people into debt, thanks to the development of a real financial structure with tools and products that have enabled an hypertrophic growth of the mass of money and debts?" This is a question posed by Andrea Baranes in his book *Dobbiamo restituire fiducia ai mercati. Falso!* (We Must Restore Confidence to the Markets. False!) where he explains the mechanism of the subprime mortgage crisis that originated in the United States and then spread throughout the world.[8]

We could at least start questioning, for example, the system of "derivatives"—that is, the financial contracts that originate as insurance against risks, offering the right or the ability to buy, sell, or trade an entity (called "underlying") at a precise date in the future and that in 99 percent of cases do not end with the delivery of an asset, but only on the future value of the underlying entity.

The derivative can change value because the underlying value changes—for example, the value of wheat—but it can also change only for financial reasons. For example, a derivative on wheat may increase in value because the market is on a temporary rise, because a large investor decided to enter the derivatives market, or because a speculative wave brings up the value of derivatives. These financial factors affect the price of derivatives, which in turn influence also that of whatever underlies them—in our case, wheat. This means that the commodity market follows the directions of the derivatives market. Thus the price of wheat does not increase or decrease as a result of famines, weather-related events, and so on, but is influenced by that of derivatives on wheat that have become the main assets traded on financial markets.

Therefore, the real economy—which includes the lives of those who cultivate, manufacture, sell, and buy wheat—ends up becoming a tool in the service of finance, and not vice versa.

Are we sure that this system will not actually end up violating the laws of the free market and competition in which the same financial markets say they are grounded? "Today the price of wheat," observes Baranes, "or any other product, is only partially linked to its demand (the desire for bread and pasta) and supply (its production). Speculative factors affect the price and are available only to very few financial players, violating the assumed free market and competition rules. The impact affects producers as much as consumers, as both find themselves at the mercy of prices that vary independently of the performance of demand and supply. Derivatives are a prime example of how the financial system today is able to disrupt and distort even the principles of the market economy on which it should be based and which it should serve."

This is what happened, for example, with the outbreak of the financial crisis in 2008. Huge capital fled from traditional financial markets, such as stocks and bonds, in search of safer investments, such as gold and other commodities. The sudden arrival of huge amounts of capital increased the demand and, thereby, prices. In one year, between 2008 and 2009, the price of wheat and corn doubled on international markets, and then decreased significantly, after which point it increased again, and not only because of "real" events (such as the surge of demand from China). Undoubtedly, the consequences of the abrupt changes in the markets are felt concretely in the lives of millions of people and not by those few who earn fortunes betting in fractions of a second on the price of wheat. Those affected are men and women whose lives are threatened by the fact that the price of wheat and corn fluctuate dramatically from one day to the next.

Can we at least start asking whether this hypertrophy of a self-absorbed finance is one of the really critical factors of the current economic situation? Can we at least start asking whether it is desirable to introduce corrective measures to avoid devastating consequences on the functioning of the real economy and entrepreneurship? Is it right to ask whether these tools should adapt to the basic needs of the people, or whether people should adapt to the needs of financial markets, capitals with short term investment horizons, and the maximization of profit as an end in itself? Is it so inconvenient to note that, with the recession, it becomes ever more risky for banks to lend money to households and businesses (and we all know how difficult it is to get a mortgage loan!), while it is much easier and also safe to invest in the financial markets?

"On the one hand," writes Baranes, "the lack of access to credit intensifies, exacerbating the recession; on the other, more and more capital flows into the financial markets, fueling the bubble. The higher the disconnect, the more convenient and seemingly safe it is to continue to move capital from the productive economy to finance. The bubble feeds on itself." Is that true? Is it false? And if there is a grain of truth, why does no one ask how to fix the system?

The data showing the continued growth of speculative finance is not a secret. One of the headlines published in June 2013 in the Italian financial newspaper *Il Sole 24 Ore* read, "Banks are back creating 'toxic' titles," pointing out that "financial markets today are worth about $740 trillion: about $20,000 billion more than the peaks of 2007. Ten times more than the GDP of the world economy. In other words: speculative finance is back, bigger and unbridled than ever. Better yet, it never really went anywhere. The monster that in 2007 gobbled up the real economy is roaring back again." The big investment banks are "back assembling synthetic CDOs . . . for a very bleak reason: given that they are a high risk but offer good returns, investors are demanding them again. . . . It looks like we're back in 2007 all over again."[9]

The winner of the 2008 Nobel Prize for Economics and columnist for *The New York Times*, Paul Krugman, writes: "Certainly these days many vast fortunes come, not from building something, but from consistently guessing what other investors are going to do a few days, or sometimes a second or two, ahead of the pack."[10]

As we can see, there is a risk that the same speculation causes the fluctuations in the markets on which it will then gain: the more bets run on certain titles, certain countries, and certain companies, the more likely it is that the corresponding prices will go crazy. "And if prices go crazy," writes Baranes, "the chances of short-term profit increase as well. The increase of market fluctuations instability will attract new speculators . . . the current financial system is inherently unstable."

Just to give an idea of how big financialization is today, we can point to the fact that the total amount of goods and services imported and exported around the world amount to $20 trillion a year, while transactions between currencies exceed $4 trillion a day. This means that more money circulates in five days in the financial markets than in an entire year in the "real" economy.

We may ask: Is the financialization of the economy that led to the crisis a degeneration of capitalism, the result of unethical individual behavior, and the fruit of speculative bubbles and errors in the policies of the states? Or are we facing a transformation of capitalism when the expansion of the production of goods is no longer sufficient to sustain certain profits?

Joseph Stiglitz, winner of the 2010 Nobel Prize for Economics has stated: "The global economy needed ever-increasing consumption to grow; but how could this continue when the incomes of many Americans had been stagnating for so long? Americans came up with an ingenious solution: borrow and consume as if their incomes *were* growing."[11]

The "toxic" mortgage crisis of 2008, with the continuous borrowing by people unable to repay loans, however, may not be the cause but the glaring symptom of a deeper malaise linked to inequalities in the distribution of wealth. Robert B. Reich, former US Secretary of Labor, states in *Aftershock: The Next Economy and America's Future* that "Over the last three decades working families have taken home a smaller and smaller share. . . . A larger and larger portion has gone to people at the very top. This has hurt the economy. The rich don't spend as much of their earnings as the rest of us. They invest their savings wherever around the world they reap the highest return. And the rest of us, with a smaller share of the total, lack the purchasing power to keep the economy going full speed."[12]

In the face of all this, is it really so exaggerated that the pope and the Catholic Church warn against the "idolatry of money"? The aforementioned document of the Pontifical Council for Justice and Peace, on the basis of an "ethical" approach, considers it appropriate to reflect on the possibility of introducing "*taxation measures on financial transactions* with fair rates modulated in proportion to the complexity of operations, especially those made on the 'secondary' market. Such taxation would be very useful in promoting global development and sustainability according to the principles of social justice and solidarity. It could also contribute to the creation of a world reserve fund to support the economies of the countries hit by crisis as well as the recovery of their monetary and financial systems."[13]

Further, the Pontifical Council judged it also appropriate to reflect on possible "forms of recapitalization of banks with public funds, making the support conditional on 'virtuous' behaviours aimed at developing the 'real economy.'" It also called for a "definition of the two domains of ordinary credit and of Investment Banking. This distinction would allow a more effective management of the 'shadow markets' which have no controls and limits."

So who is right? Samuel Gregg, research director of the Acton Institute, when he calls for less state and more private sector to help the poor? In an interview published last August on the online newspaper *La nuova Bussola Quotidiana*, Gregg said: "We prefer to focus on the question of inequality, or on that of poverty. But I believe that the worst forms of economic inequality and poverty have originated in the collusion between the state and the business world. To break this bond, we must encourage free competition, free markets and entrepreneurship, and move incentives from the public to the private. . . . Perhaps we in the Catholic Church have not paid enough attention to the phenomenon of poverty reduction and, above all, to what generates it, and that is not state intervention, but competition and the market."[14]

Is this really the right formula, as suggested to the Catholic Church in a relatively gentle way, asking the church to finally convert to this form of capitalism and put aside some of the more troublesome pages of its social doctrine? Or is it not only legitimate but also necessary to grow a collective consciousness with regard to these issues, inviting the politicians to do their jobs and retrieve their proper role of protecting the common good and in particular those in need?

We hope the reader will excuse us for this foray into some specific financial and economic issues. But reading, or rereading, certain criticisms that have been directed toward the social pages of *Evangelii Gaudium*, one has the feeling that Francis, the first Latin American pope, in effectively presenting the church's social doctrine, has hit the mark and alarmed those who fear that certain issues will emerge again to be discussed. Further, there was no need to wait for the pope's exhortation in order to detect in Francis's ordinary magisterium some important hints and clues on specific issues. For example, on May 16, 2013, in his address to several new nonresident ambassadors to the Holy See, Francis said: "We have created new idols. The worship of the golden calf of old . . . has found a new and heartless image in the cult of money and the dictatorship of an economy which is faceless and lacking any truly humane goal. The worldwide financial and economic crisis seems to highlight their distortions and above all the gravely deficient human perspective, which reduces man to one of his needs alone, namely, consumption. Worse yet, human beings themselves are nowadays considered as consumer goods which can be used and thrown away. We have started a throw-away culture. This tendency is seen on the level of individuals and whole societies; and it is being promoted!"[15]

"In circumstances like these," continued Francis, "solidarity, which is the treasure of the poor, is often considered counterproductive, opposed to the logic of finance and the economy. While the income of a minority is increasing exponentially, that of the majority is crumbling. This imbalance results from ideologies which uphold the absolute autonomy of markets and financial speculation, and thus deny the right of control to States, which are themselves charged with providing for the common good."

According to Francis, the total autonomy of the markets is a form of tyranny: "A new, invisible and at times virtual, tyranny is established, one which unilaterally and irremediably imposes its own laws and rules. Moreover, indebtedness and credit distance countries from their real economy and citizens from their real buying power. Added to this, as if it were needed, is widespread corruption and selfish fiscal evasion which have taken on worldwide dimensions. The will to power and of possession has become limitless."

Francis concluded the speech calling for a "financial reform along ethical lines that would produce in its turn an economic reform to benefit everyone. This would nevertheless require a courageous change of attitude on the part of political leaders."

Another example, significant and absolutely clear in content, was on June 20, 2013, when the Bishop of Rome received in audience the participants in a conference of the Food and Agriculture Organization of the United Nations (FAO): "The human person and human dignity risk being turned into vague abstractions in the face of issues like the use of force, war, malnutrition, marginalization, violence, the violation of basic liberties, and financial speculation, which presently affects the price of food, treating it like any other merchandise and overlooking its primary function."[16]

"Our task," added Francis, "is to continue to insist, in the present international context, that the human person and human dignity are not simply catchwords, but pillars for creating shared rules and structures capable of passing beyond purely pragmatic or technical approaches in order to eliminate divisions and to bridge existing differences."

With this in mind, and following in this direction, the pope concluded: "There is a need to oppose the shortsighted economic interests and the mentality of power of a relative few who exclude the majority of the world's peoples, generating poverty and marginalization and causing a breakdown in society. There is likewise a need to combat the corruption which creates privileges for some and injustices for many others."

Finally, we must not forget the pope's words pronounced after the exhortation *Evangelii Gaudium*, such as this passage from the message for the World Day of Peace on January 1, 2014, when Francis observed: "The grave financial and economic crises of the present time—which find their origin in the progressive distancing of man from God and from his neighbour, in the greedy pursuit of material goods on the one hand, and in the impoverishment of interpersonal and community relations on the other—have pushed man to seek satisfaction, happiness and security in consumption and earnings out of all proportion to the principles of a sound economy."[17]

"The succession of economic crises," added Francis, "should lead to a timely rethinking of our models of economic development and to a change in lifestyles. Today's crisis, even with its serious implications for people's lives, can also provide us with a fruitful opportunity to rediscover the virtues of prudence, temperance, justice and strength. These virtues can help us to overcome difficult moments and to recover the fraternal bonds which join us one to another, with deep confidence that human beings need and are capable of something greater than maximizing their individual interest. Above all, these virtues are necessary for building and preserving a society in accord with human dignity."

chapter 7

AMERICAN THEOCON CRITICISM . . . OF BENEDICT XVI?

> *This concentration of power and might, the characteristic mark,*
> *as it were, of contemporary economic life, is the fruit that the*
> *unlimited freedom of struggle among competitors has of its own*
> *nature produced, and which lets only the strongest survive; and*
> *this is often the same as saying, those who fight the most violently,*
> *those who give least heed to their conscience.*
>
> —Pius XI, *Quadragesimo Anno*

We would be remiss, however, after going through some of the most flagrant accusations leveled against Pope Francis, to forget an important detail: not many years ago, similar attacks from American neocon and theocon circles were also raised against Pope Benedict XVI. In fact, on June 29, 2009, Benedict XVI signed his third encyclical, *Caritas in Veritate*, which dealt primarily with social issues. At over one hundred pages, it was essentially an update on Paul VI's *Populorum Progressio* (1967) and John Paul II's *Centesimus Annus* (1991). The world had changed between 1991 and 2009, and there was need for a fresh new look on specific issues. The encyclical, whose publication had been delayed to allow the inclusion of a few thoughts on the economic and financial crisis, calls for a national economic development of countries to be implemented along three inseparably linked directives: responsibility, solidarity, and subsidiarity.

The pope's document met widespread acclaim but also some criticism. According to some, different topics were presented without taking a clear position, leaving room for ambivalence. With regard to globalization, for example, there were those who found that the document was attentive to the "great problems of injustice in the development of peoples," but also that "growth has taken place, and it continues to be a positive factor that has lifted billions of people out of misery." Coincidentally, similar criticism was moved against Benedict's successor.

But the strongest criticism was over the passages dealing with the markets and globalization; and, surprisingly, those critics were from the "right"—namely, those who have a clear and especially positive idea of markets and globalization. The paragraphs that received most of the criticism are the ones that follow.[1]

Benedict XVI writes: "The global market has stimulated first and foremost, on the part of rich countries, a search for areas in which to outsource production at low cost. . . . Consequently, the market has prompted new forms of competition between States as they seek to attract foreign businesses to set up production centres, by means of a variety of instruments, including favourable fiscal regimes and deregulation of the labour market. These processes have led to a *downsizing of social security systems*."

Further, the pope adds: "Through the combination of social and economic change, *trade union organizations* experience greater difficulty in carrying out their task of representing the interests of workers." And then, "The global context in which work takes place also demands that national labour unions . . . turn their attention to those outside their membership, and in particular to workers in developing countries"

A passage on foreign trade follows: we must "give serious attention to the damage that can be caused to one's home country by the transfer abroad of capital purely for personal advantage," and "there is no reason to deny that a certain amount of capital can do good, if invested abroad rather than at home."

About a month after the release of the encyclical, the aforementioned Michael Novak—together with other leading American

Catholic neoconservatives such as the late Richard John Neu-
haus and George Weigel—had his say in the online pages of *First
Things*.[2] Novak's ideas are well known. For years he has proposed
his "democratic capitalism" as the political and economic system
most compatible with Christianity, especially Catholicism. To
the Catholic world Novak has always presented himself as an
opponent of liberation theology, considered clearly molded on
Marxism, to convince Catholics to accept in all respects "market
capitalism." Novak has always deemed himself capable of reading
within the papal texts the theory of market capitalism, especially
in encyclicals. But then he overlooks the same papal condemnations of those mechanisms of debt and monopolization with
which different developing countries must deal. Not surprisingly,
in a comment on John Paul II's *Centesimus Annus* that appeared
in *National Review*, Novak wrote, "If in Vatican II, Rome accepted
American ideas of religious liberty, in *Centesimus Annus* Rome has
assimilated American ideas of economic liberty."[3]

Thus, in 2009 Novak stood up to make his remarks on Pope
Benedict's encyclical. And the headline for the Italian edition of
his article indicates specifically what and how Novak intended to
attack: "Too much *Caritas*, too little *Veritas*. Benedict XVI's new
encyclical: between right intuitions and (involuntary) omissions."

Novak begins warily. It becomes clear that he would rather
attack the papal text more explicitly, but at the beginning he
remains cautious. Then, slowly, he starts to come into the open
and writes, "The staff work [for the encyclical] has been rather
poor," and then he continues: "For myself, though, I love best the
starting point in *caritas*," because "watching Benedict XVI write
about *caritas* so beautifully brings me immense satisfaction." But
then comes the jab:

> In all candor, however, if we hold each sentence of *Caritas in
> Veritate* up to analysis in the light of empirical truth about events
> in the field of political economy since 1967, we will find that it is
> not nearly so full in its *veritas* as in its *caritas*. For instance, the
> benefits for the poor achieved through the spread of economic
> enterprise and markets (capitalism is for some too unpleasant a

word to use) should be more resoundingly attended to. In 1970, for instance, the mortality age of men and women in Bangladesh was 44.6 years old, but by 2005 it had risen to 63. Think what a joy and what vigor such increased longevity means to individual families. Similarly, infant mortality rate (deaths per 1,000 live births) in Bangladesh in 1970 was 152, or 15.2 percent. By 2005 this average had been brought down to just 57.2, or a little less than 6 percent. Again, what pain this lifts from ordinary mothers and fathers, and what joy it brings. There is surely more to do to raise health standards for Bangladeshi. But the progress just in this past thirty years is unprecedented in world history. There are many more omissions of fact, questionable insinuations, and unintentional errors strewn through this encyclical. . . . Every deficiency of *veritas* injures *caritas*. That is the beautiful and powerful linkage in this encyclical.

In short, Benedict XVI's text, according to the American scholar, is too reticent. It fails to recognize, with due emphasis and in length, the importance of capitalism for the advancement of the poor.

But Novak was not the only one to criticize Benedict XVI's social encyclical. One of the main biographers of both John Paul II and Benedict XV, American public commentator George Weigel, followed suit. On July 7, 2009, Weigel wrote an article titled "*Caritas in Veritate* in Gold and Red" for *National Review*.[4] According to Weigel, chair in Catholic Studies of the Ethics & Public Policy Center, *Caritas in Veritate* is a "hybrid" creature—he compares it to a platypus—where one can find and highlight with a yellow marker the passages related to Benedict's authentic thought while underlining in red the "incorrect" ones—those developed by the Pontifical Council for Justice and Peace and vitiated by an entrenched and naïve third-world outlook, considered typical of conciliar thinking.

Weigel was therefore critical of the work that, in his view, was put into the preparation of the encyclical:

The Pontifical Council for Justice and Peace, which imagines itself the curial keeper of the flame of authentic Catholic social teaching, prepared a draft, which was duly sent to Pope John

Paul II—who had already had a bad experience with the conventionally *gauchiste* and not-very-original thinking at Justice and Peace during the preparation of the 1987 social encyclical, *Sollicitudo Rei Socialis*. John Paul shared the proposed draft with colleagues in whose judgment he reposed trust; one prominent intellectual who had long been in conversation with the Pope told him that the draft was unacceptable, in that it simply did not reflect the way the global economy of the post–Cold War world worked.

So John Paul dumped the Justice and Peace draft and crafted an encyclical that was a fitting commemoration of *Rerum Novarum*. For *Centesimus Annus* not only summarized deftly the intellectual structure of Catholic social doctrine since Leo XIII; it proposed a bold trajectory for the further development of this unique body of thought, emphasizing the priority of culture in the threefold free society (free economy, democratic polity, vibrant public moral culture). By stressing human creativity as the source of the wealth of nations, *Centesimus Annus* also displayed a far more empirically acute reading of the economic signs of the times than was evident in the default positions at Justice and Peace. Moreover, *Centesimus Annus* jettisoned the idea of a "Catholic third way" that was somehow "between" or "beyond" or "above" capitalism and socialism—a favorite dream of Catholics ranging from G. K. Chesterton to John A. Ryan and Ivan Illich.

In short, according to Weigel, John Paul II had finally shown to the Catholic Church that capitalism, as we know it, was the best, the most appropriate, and the most *Catholic* system. And from this instrumental perspective, intended to sanction the indissoluble alliance between the church and the free market, Benedict XVI's encyclical already appeared to be a step backward.

As a result, Weigel sought to deconstruct the magisterial text, separating what he believed was Ratzinger's authentic thought from the passages prepared by his collaborators of the Pontifical Council for Justice and Peace.

Weigel wrote: "But then there are those passages to be marked in red—the passages that reflect Justice and Peace ideas and approaches that Benedict evidently believed he had to try and accommodate." Weigel explains that the passages on "gratuitousness" and "gift" certainly would fit better in a spiritual context, and not in a socioeconomic one. Those on a "world political authority" could have been justified at the time of John XXIII, but less so today.

Weigel concludes by writing: "If those burrowed into the intellectual and institutional woodwork at the Pontifical Council for Justice and Peace imagine *Caritas in Veritate* as reversing the rout they believe they suffered with *Centesimus Annus*, and if they further imagine *Caritas in Veritate* setting Catholic social doctrine on a completely new, *Populorum Progressio*–defined course (as one Justice and Peace consultor has already said), they are likely to be disappointed. The incoherence of the Justice and Peace sections of the new encyclical is so deep, and the language in some cases so impenetrable, that what the defenders of *Populorum Progressio* may think to be a new sounding of the trumpet is far more like the warbling of an untuned piccolo."

Thus we have seen two leaders of American Catholic conservatism who had openly criticized Benedict's encyclical. Because if in John Paul II's *Centesimus Annus* capitalism somehow passed the test, Benedict's document remains more cautious and advances several criticisms. And for the two American intellectuals that is unacceptable. They probably did not expect such a text, especially from Benedict. Hence we have their attempt to attribute the encyclical to a kind of conspiracy of the Pontifical Council for Justice and Peace, which at that time was headed by Cardinal Renato Raffaele Martino—the "revenge of Justice and Peace," as the subtitle to Weigel's article puts it. A conspiracy that, to be fair, would have to be proven first.

Today, no one remembers these criticisms of Benedict XVI, when the German pope dared venture out of familiar territories and from the organic reading of his own pontificate that his supporters had built. In effect, today the misleading contrast between Benedict and his successor is more prevalent. It is an opposition based not so much on elements of discontinuity—always and obviously evident when comparing different pontificates—but rather on a hostility that certain circles, even within the Catholic world, manifest toward Francis's testimony and teaching.

Returning to those accusations made against Benedict's social encyclical, a few months after the American conservative criticisms, a response arrived from Cardinal Martino himself, one of Novak and Weigel's main "suspects":

> The criticism from some American circles to Benedict XVI's encyclical does not surprise me that much . . . the church, as its *Compendium of the Social Doctrine* makes clear, does not forget and cannot forget that scientific and technological progress, as well as the globalization of markets, which can be a source of development and progress, however, exposes workers to the risk of being exploited by the mechanisms of the economy and the unbridled pursuit of productivity. The Church does not forget, and cannot forget, that the same right to private property is subordinated to the principle of the universal destination of goods. This is a principle that applies to financial, technical, intellectual, and personal goods as well. The mechanisms of the economic system must be at the service of humanity and not of illicit exploitation and speculation. It seems to me that these criticisms from well-known circles in the United States end up revealing a desire to have the pope say what those same circles would like to hear, to support and legitimize their positions, downplaying or censoring what the magisterium of the Church says that it is not in line with those positions, for example, on globalization, the market, and the defense and protection of creation.

These pages dedicated to Pope Benedict XVI's encyclical *Caritas in Veritate* show, therefore, that there is the constant attempt to have the Catholic Church say what others would like her to say, or to have her impart her blessing on one's own economic systems and worldviews. By looking back to what happened in 2009, are we still surprised by the taunts thrown at Francis, who, unlike his predecessor, is also "guilty"—in the eyes of certain capitalist think tanks—of coming from South America and of speaking more frequently of the poor?

chapter 8

WELFARE TO BE DISMANTLED?

> *The common good requires the* social well-being. . . .
> *Development is the epitome of all social duties. Certainly, it is*
> *the proper function of authority to arbitrate, in the name of the*
> *common good, between various particular interests; but it should*
> *make accessible to each what is needed to lead a truly human*
> *life: food, clothing, health, work, education and culture, suitable*
> *information, the right to establish a family, and so on.*
>
> —*Catechism of the Catholic Church*, no. 1908

"The social state of right and, in particular, the fundamental right to employment should not be dismantled." In his speech to the participants in the plenary assembly of the Pontifical Council for Justice and Peace, led by Cardinal Peter Turkson and held in the Clementine Hall of the Apostolic Palace on October 2, 2014, Francis offered a glimpse of his social gospel. "[The social state of right] is a fundamental good in regard to dignity, to the formation of a family, to the realization of the common good and of peace," and for the pope, it "cannot be considered a variable dependent on financial and monetary markets."[1]

The pope also recalled that the plenary assembly of the Pontifical Council, "coincides with the fifth anniversary of the promulgation of the encyclical *Caritas in Veritate*, a fundamental document for the evangelization of society, which offers valuable guidelines for the presence of Catholics in society, in institutions, in the economy, in finance and in politics. *Caritas in Veritate*," continued Francis, "called attention to the benefits but also the dangers of globalization, when it is not oriented to the good of peoples. If globalization has notably increased the aggregate wealth of the whole and of numerous individual States, it has also exacerbated the gap among the various social groups, creating inequality and new poverty in the very countries considered the wealthiest."

"One of the aspects of today's economic system," added the pope, "is the exploitation of the international disparity in labour costs, which weighs on thousands of people who live on less than two dollars a day. This imbalance not only fails to respect the dignity of those who provide low-cost labour, but it destroys the sources of employment in those regions in which it is the most protected. This raises the issue of creating mechanisms for the protection of the right to employment, as well as of the environment, in the presence of a growing consumerist ideology, which does not show responsibility in conflicts with cities and with Creation." In other words, welfare and labor protection are not variables to be abolished in times of crisis, as is often asserted by some spheres of financial capitalism.

"The growth of inequality and poverty," said Francis, "undermines inclusive and participatory democracy at risk which always presupposes an economy and an equitable and nonexclusive market. It is a question, therefore, of overcoming the structural causes of inequality and poverty." Francis then pointed out the "three fundamental instruments for the social inclusion of the most needy: education, access to health care, and employment for all."

"In other words," added Francis, "the social state of right and, in particular, the fundamental right to employment should not be dismantled. This cannot be considered a variable dependent on financial and monetary markets. It is a fundamental good in regard to dignity, to the formation of a family, to the realization of the common good and of peace. Education, work and access to health care for all are key elements for development and the just distribution of goods, for the attainment of social justice, for membership in society, and for free and responsible participation in political life."

Then, Francis stated: "Views that claim to increase profitability, at the cost of restricting the labour market, thereby creating new exclusions, are not in conformity with an economy at the service of man and of the common good, with an inclusive and participatory democracy."

The pope also addressed the issue of "the persistent inequalities in economic sectors, in wages, in commercial and speculative banks, including institutions and global problems," adding that "It requires, on one hand, significant *reforms* that provide for the redistribution of the wealth produced and universalization of free markets at the service of families, and, on the other, the redistribution of sovereignty, on both the national and supranational planes."

Finally, Pope Francis recalled that *Caritas in Veritate* called us "to regard the present social issue as an environmental question. In particular, it remarked on the link between environmental ecology and human ecology, between the former and life's ethics."

"The principle of *Caritas in Veritate* is extremely relevant today. A love full of truth," added Francis, "is in fact the foundation on which to build the peace that is particularly desired and necessary today for the good of all. With this principle, dangerous fanaticisms, conflicts over the possession of resources, migrations of biblical dimensions, unrelenting epidemics of hunger and poverty, human trafficking, social and economic injustices and disparities, and unequal access to collective goods can be overcome."

These are clear words that leave no room for misunderstandings of interpretation. Bishop Mario Toso, secretary of the Pontifical Council for Justice and Peace, clarifies the proposal launched by Francis in *Evangelii Gaudium* for "a more inclusive economy."[2] "Globalization," observed Toso, "has set in motion a process of convergence between the average income of the poorest countries and the richest countries, but at the same time, it has increased the inequalities between different parts of the world population. The two phenomena are the product of the same revolution. The market is becoming globalized while increasing the gaps in schooling levels, and by bringing about intense competition between low cost workers in low-income countries

with workers with high wages in high-income countries." Therefore, we are "going through a long transition that is promising,
although problematic and complex, which will hopefully lead
from the old world, segmented within national borders, to a
new world populated by a single human family." For this reason, Toso believes that "the economic problem that economists
have traditionally dealt with is only one of the dimensions of the
problem. We have to ensure that the creation of economic value
is environmentally sustainable."

There is therefore an environmental dimension, in addition
to the economic. Francis wants to ensure that there are no "dramatic financial crises" as well as "no disparity between GDP and
well-being." "The apostolic exhortation *Evangelii Gaudium*," reiterated Toso, "offers really exciting perspectives, but it should be
studied and translated into an economic plan, because distorting
interpretations have emerged accusing the pope of Marxism."
Toso added that it is necessary to explain that "the proposal of
a 'more inclusive economy' does not imply a rejection of the
market economy; if anything, it means the valorization of it and
of its positive aspects. . . . The 'economy that kills' to which
Francis alluded—and unfortunately there were many cases of
entrepreneurs and laid off workers who committed suicide—is
not the whole economy, but one that idolizes money; one that
considers work a variable dependent on financial and monetary
mechanisms."[3]

Andrea Riccardi, founder of the Community of Sant'Egidio
and a historian of the modern church and contemporary art,
is convinced that Francis wants to "elicit, through preaching, a
change in lifestyle and consumption." Thus "as bishop of Buenos
Aires, and now that he is in Rome, the pope opposes the culture of
waste." For Francis "the poor are the heart of Christianity and not
an appendage of the Gospel." As a case in point, at the Angelus
of Sunday, August 5, 2014, the pope said that to turn away and
feel uncomfortable in the presence of the poor means to follow
"the logic of the world."

"Francis's gospel is evangelical, not social. Often, in the two
thousand year history of the church, the poor and the social

question were considered as appendages of Christianity," says Professor Riccardi. "On the contrary, Pope Francis reiterates that the poor are at the heart of Christianity; so to look the other way is like giving up one's heart. For Francis, to look to the poor is not exclusivist, but rather the premise of a universal outlook. It is something that we must begin to understand. Not only is war the mother of many forms of poverty, but hunger and poverty are mothers of war and violence."[4]

It is an underlying theological choice. "In the poor, Francis sees the presence of Jesus," claims Riccardi. "To carry out his mission, Francis starts from the poor in a very concrete and not ideological way, and in so doing lashes out against the economic, political, and social systems with prophetic power. In the storm of the crisis in Argentina, he never experienced the ideological temptation of revolutionary Marxism. At the same time, however, Jorge Mario Bergoglio never fell into line with that wing of the church in Argentina that justified inequality and exploitation. Francis is placing a sensitive and compassionate church of Rome on the frontiers of the discomfort."

Besides, "even before he became bishop, Bergoglio was very sensitive to the poor," emphasizes the founder of the community of Sant'Egidio. "That stems from the centrality of the gospel message in his life. In the gospel, in fact, the poor, the hungry, have a very significant role," points out Riccardi. "Francis is the key to understanding the primacy of the human over the economic. Bergoglio has always judged capitalism by its fruits, and it is from this absence of prejudices that Bergoglio gets his freedom from ideology. Through his preaching, he intends to elicit a movement against the consumer culture of waste. In short, as Father Joseph Wresinski titled one of his books, the poor *are* the church."

In this way, "Francis demonstrates to an often distracted world public opinion, that the fight against poverty and hunger is a decisive fact and a reality that we constantly have to face. Not only is it an emergency, but, unfortunately, a dramatic constant in the history of our time."

chapter 9

THE PROTECTION OF CREATION

*We are the heirs of earlier generations, and we reap benefits from
the efforts of our contemporaries; we are under obligation to all
men. Therefore we cannot disregard the welfare of those who will
come after us to increase the human family.*

—Paul VI, *Populorum Progressio*

For the first pope who chose the name of the *Poverello* of Assisi,
the protection of creation is a priority. On June 5, 2013, on the
occasion of the World Environment Day, an event sponsored by
the United Nations, Pope Francis addressed the general audience
on the theme of environmental protection.[1] "My thoughts go to
the first pages of the Bible, to the Book of Genesis, where it says
that God puts men and women on the earth to till it and keep
it," said the pontiff. "And these questions occur to me: What does
cultivating and preserving the earth mean? Are we truly cultivating and caring for creation? Or are we exploiting and neglecting
it? The verb 'cultivate' reminds me of the care a farmer takes to
ensure that his land will be productive and that his produce will
be shared. What great attention, enthusiasm and dedication!
Cultivating and caring for creation is an instruction of God which
he gave not only at the beginning of history, but has also given to
each one of us; it is part of his plan; it means making the world
increase with responsibility, transforming it so that it may be a
garden, an inhabitable place for us all."

Francis quoted his predecessor Benedict XVI, recalling that
several times Benedict called upon all to "this task entrusted to

us by God the Creator," which requires us "to grasp the pace and the logic of creation." "Instead," added Francis, "we are often guided by the pride of dominating, possessing, manipulating and exploiting; we do not 'preserve' the earth, we do not respect it, we do not consider it as a freely-given gift to look after. We are losing our attitude of wonder, of contemplation, of listening to creation and thus we no longer manage to interpret in it what Benedict XVI calls 'the rhythm of the love-story between God and man.'"

"Why does this happen?" asked Francis. "[Because] we think and live horizontally, we have drifted away from God, we no longer read his signs." Francis then explained that "'cultivating and caring' do not only entail the relationship between us and the environment, between man and creation. They also concern human relations. The popes have spoken of a *human ecology*, closely connected with *environmental ecology*. We are living in a time of crisis; we see it in the environment, but above all we see it in men and women. The human person is in danger: this much is certain—the human person is in danger today, hence the urgent need for human ecology!"

"And the peril," added the pope, "is grave, because the cause of the problem is not superficial but deeply rooted. It is not merely a question of economics but of ethics and anthropology. The Church has frequently stressed this; and many are saying: yes, it is right, it is true . . . but the system continues unchanged since what dominates are the dynamics of an economy and a finance that are lacking in ethics."

Francis then, speaking more spontaneously, added, "It is no longer man who commands, but money, money, cash commands. And God our Father gave us the task of protecting the earth—not for money, but for ourselves: for men and women. We have this task!"

"Nevertheless," he continued, "men and women are sacrificed to the idols of profit and consumption: it is the 'culture of waste.' If a computer breaks it is a tragedy, but poverty, the needs and dramas of so many people end up being considered normal." Therefore, "if on a winter's night, here on the Via Ottaviano—for example—someone dies, that is not news. If there are children in so many parts of the world who have nothing to eat, that is not news, it seems normal. It cannot be so! And yet these things enter into normality: that some homeless people should freeze to death on the street—this doesn't make news. On the contrary, when the stock market drops 10 points in some cities, it constitutes a tragedy. Someone who dies is not news, but lowering income by 10 points is a tragedy! In this way people are thrown aside as if they were trash."

"This 'culture of waste,'" warns Francis, "tends to become a common mentality that infects everyone. Human life, the person, are no longer seen as a primary value to be respected and safeguarded. . . . This culture of waste has also made us insensitive to wasting and throwing out excess foodstuffs, which is especially condemnable when, in every part of the world, unfortunately, many people and families suffer hunger and malnutrition. There was a time when our grandparents were very careful not to throw away any left over food. Consumerism has induced us to be accustomed to excess and to the daily waste of food, whose value, which goes far beyond mere financial parameters, we are no longer able to judge correctly."

Francis then recalled that "whenever food is thrown out it is as if it were stolen from the table of the poor, from the hungry! I ask everyone to reflect on the problem of the loss and waste of food, to identify ways and approaches which, by seriously dealing with this problem, convey solidarity and sharing with the underprivileged."

"A few days ago, on the feast of Corpus Christi," continued Francis,

> we read the account of the miracle of the multiplication of the loaves. Jesus fed the multitude with five loaves and two fish. And the end of this passage is important: "and all ate and were satisfied. And they took up what was left over, twelve baskets of broken pieces" (Luke 9:17). Jesus asked the disciples to ensure that nothing was wasted: nothing thrown out! And there is this fact of 12 baskets: why 12? What does it mean? Twelve is the number of the tribes of Israel, it represents symbolically the whole people. And this tells us that when the food was shared fairly, with solidarity, no one was deprived of what he needed, every community could meet the needs of its poorest members.

Therefore, explained Francis, "human and environmental ecology go hand in hand. I would therefore like us all to make the serious commitment to respect and care for creation, to pay attention to every person, to combat the culture of waste and of throwing out so as to foster a culture of solidarity and encounter."

On January 13, 2014, in the Sala Regia of the Apostolic Palace, in his first address to members of the diplomatic corps accredited to the Holy See, Francis warned that we must respect nature, because when she "is mistreated she never forgives!"[2] Earlier, he said, "I wish to mention another threat to peace, which arises from the greedy exploitation of environmental resources."

Remembering the victims of Typhoon Haiyan, which hit the Philippines in November 2013, causing more than 5,000 victims, the pope wanted also to emphasize the theme of environmental protection as the protection of creation: "We have also witnessed the devastating effects of several recent natural disasters. . . . Here too what is crucial is responsibility on the part of all in pursuing, in a spirit of fraternity, policies respectful of this earth which is our common home." Because, said Francis, recalling a popular saying: "God always forgives, we sometimes forgive, but when nature—creation—is mistreated, she never forgives!" At the Angelus of Sunday, February 9, 2014, Francis returned to the theme of protecting and respecting creation. His words were motivated by the bad weather that hit various parts of the world. The pope prayed "for those who are suffering damage and discomforts due to natural disasters, in many countries," and noted that nature "challenges us to be sympathetic and attentive to protecting creation, and to prevent, as much as possible, the most serious of consequences."[3]

Pope Francis had already expressed his concern for creation in his homily during the Mass for the beginning of his pontificate, on March 19, 2013, when he urged not only Christians but all men and women to protect "all creation, the beauty of the created world," and to respect "each of God's creatures and respecting the environment in which we live."[4] Also, on May 21, 2014, during the general audience, Francis reiterated his warning: "We must protect creation for it is a gift which the Lord has given us." Then he launched a strong warning: "This must be our attitude to creation: guard it for if we destroy creation, creation will destroy us!"[5]

The pope also recalled human responsibility when he said that "the gift of knowledge helps us not to fall into attitudes of excess or error. The first lies in the risk of considering ourselves the masters of creation. Creation is not some possession that we can lord over for our own pleasure; nor, even less, is it the property of only some people, the few: creation is a gift, it is the marvellous gift that God has given us, *so that we will take care of it and harness it for the benefit of all, always with great respect and gratitude.*" Francis then urged the faithful to be the "guardians of creation. When we exploit creation, we destroy that sign of God's love. To destroy creation is to say to God: 'I don't care.' And this is not good: this is sin. Custody of creation is precisely custody of God's gift. . . . Don't forget that!"

On June 18, 2015, the Vatican unveiled Francis's second encyclical, *Laudato Sì*, subtitled "On Care for Our Common Home." It is a historic addition to the church's body of social teaching.

The principle contribution of the new document is its criticism of the current model of economic development, which seems to have pushed the world and all that it contains toward an abyss. The ecological emergency, it argues, is inseparable from the structural problems of poverty and underdevelopment, because "the present world system is certainly unsustainable from a number of points of view."[6]

Francis writes:

> The economy accepts every advance in technology with a view to profit, without concern for its potentially negative impact on human beings. Finance overwhelms the real economy. . . . Some circles maintain that current economics and technology will solve all environmental problems, and argue, in popular and non-technical terms, that the problems of global hunger and poverty will be resolved simply by market growth. . . . Yet by itself the market cannot guarantee integral human development and social inclusion.

The pope insists that "politics must not be subject to the economy, nor should the economy be subject to the dictates of an efficiency-driven paradigm of technocracy. . . . Saving banks at any cost, making the public pay the price, foregoing a firm commitment to reviewing and reforming the entire system, only reaffirms the absolute power of a financial system, a power which has no future and will only give rise to new crises."

He invites readers "to reject a magical conception of the market, which would suggest that problems can be solved simply by an increase in the profits of companies or individuals. . . . Given the insatiable and irresponsible growth produced over many decades, we need also to think of containing growth by setting some reasonable limits" and "accept[ing] decreased growth in some parts of the world, in order to provide resources for other places to experience healthy growth." Francis observes, "The principle of the maximization of profits, frequently isolated from other considerations, reflects a misunderstanding of the very concept of the economy" and, today, "some economic sectors exercise more power than states themselves."

With the same courage he displayed two years earlier, when he questioned the hypocrisy of powerful leaders who speak of peace at the same time they make lucrative backroom weapons deals with guerrillas and terrorists, Francis identifies the links between the financial crises, the epochal migration of peoples, and wars for the control of oil and water. He offers timely and strong criticism—difficult even for politicians on the left to hear—of a system in which "finance overwhelms the real economy" and "our politics are subject to technology and finance." It is a system in which "economic interests easily end up trumping the common good and manipulating information so that their own plans will not be affected." At the same time, we are handed certain pronouncements financed by large multinational energy corporations that suggest the environmental alarm is a lie, that the system in which we live is the best we can hope for, and that to think of changing it would be folly.

The pope does not propose a romantic idealism or a return to the caves, nor does he predict catastrophe. Rather, he offers concrete and practical solutions at all levels, with realism and a broad perspective, making connections we might otherwise miss or ignore. Starting from the goodness of creation as a gift we must "till" and "keep" for future generations, he calls us to break free of immobility, helplessness, and disinterest. Using words of Benedict XVI that had been hastily filed away by many self-styled Ratzingerian intellectuals, Francis calls for greater sobriety, reduced consumption, and the establishment of an international political authority capable of limiting the obvious dominance of markets. *Laudato Sì* calls for a commitment shared by everyone. It proposes lifestyle changes and supports grassroots movements, such as those of consumers who make judgments about their portfolios based in part on the sustainability of companies in which they invest.

chapter 10

LAND, HOUSING, AND WORK

*"But since manufacturing and industry have so rapidly pervaded
and occupied countless regions, not only in the countries called
new, but also in the realms of the Far East that have been civilized
from antiquity, the number of the non-owning working poor has
increased enormously and their groans cry to God from the earth.
Added to them is the huge army of rural wage workers, pushed
to the lowest level of existence and deprived of all hope of ever
acquiring 'some property in land.'"*

—Pius XI, *Quadragesimo Anno*

On October 28, 2014, in the Old Synod Hall, Pope Francis welcomed over two hundred participants at the world meeting of popular movements organized by the Pontifical Council for Justice and Peace.[1] He said that "empty promises" cannot be the answer to the poverty in which many people are reduced around the world: farmers (*campesinos*); temporary workers and migrants; cardboard collectors and street vendors. But it is important to fight "against the structural causes of poverty." This eloquent and personal speech is worth rereading. Pope Francis read it in Spanish and announced that in the encyclical on ecology, *Laudato Sì*, which has recently been released, the popular movements' "concerns" will have their place in it as well.

The meeting at the Vatican "is a sign, it is a great sign, for you have brought a reality that is often silenced into the presence of God, the Church and all peoples. The poor not only suffer injustice, they also struggle against it!"

Francis said that the poor "are not satisfied with empty promises, with alibis or excuses. Nor do you wait with arms crossed
for NGOs to help, for welfare schemes or paternalistic solutions
that never arrive; or if they do, then it is with a tendency to
anaesthetize or to domesticate . . . and this is rather perilous."
"The poor," added Francis, "are no longer waiting. You want to
be protagonists. You get organized, study, work, issue demands
and, above all, practice that very special solidarity that exists
among those who suffer, among the poor, and that our civilization seems to have forgotten or would strongly prefer to forget."

"Solidarity is a word that is not always well received. In certain circumstances it has become a dirty word, something one
dares not say. However, it is a word that means much more than
an occasional gesture of generosity. It means thinking and acting
in terms of community. It means that the lives of all take priority
over the appropriation of goods by a few."

"It also means fighting," continued Francis, "against the structural causes of poverty and inequality; of the lack of work, land
and housing; and of the denial of social and labour rights. It
means confronting the destructive effects of the empire of money:
forced dislocation, painful emigration, human trafficking, drugs,
war, violence and all those realities that many of you suffer and
that we are all called upon to transform. Solidarity, understood
in its deepest sense, is a way of making history, and this is what
the popular movements are doing."

Francis then stressed that the meeting with the popular movements was not "shaped by an ideology. . . . You do not work
with abstract ideas; you work with realities such as those I just
mentioned and many others that you have told me about. You
have your feet in the mud, you are up to your elbows in flesh-
and-blood reality. You carry the smell of your neighborhood, your
people, your struggle! We want your voices to be heard—voices
that are rarely heard. No doubt this is because your voices cause
embarrassment, no doubt it is because your cries are bother-
some, no doubt because people are afraid of the change that you
seek. However, without your presence, without truly going to the
fringes, the good proposals and projects we often hear about at

international conferences remain stuck in the realm of ideas and wishful thinking."

Therefore, we cannot face the scandal of poverty by promoting strategies of containment that only "tranquilize the poor and render them tame and inoffensive." Francis also noted how "sad it is when we find, behind allegedly altruistic works, the other being reduced to passivity or being negated; or worse still, we find hidden personal agendas or commercial interests. 'Hypocrites' is what Jesus would say to those responsible."

The pope instead commended the movement of peoples, especially their young and poorest members, hoping that the "promising breeze" becomes a "cyclone of hope" and recalling how the yearning for social justice and the overcoming of what *Evangelii Gaudium* called "inequality," "should be within everyone's reach, namely *land, housing and work*. However, nowadays, it is sad to see that land, housing and work are ever more distant for the majority." "It is strange," noted Francis, "if I talk about this, some say that the Pope is communist. They do not understand that love for the poor is at the centre of the Gospel. Land, housing and work, what you struggle for, are sacred rights. To make this claim is nothing unusual; it is the social teaching of the Church."

Land was one of the key points of the meeting. "At the beginning of creation," said the pope,

> God created man and woman, stewards of his work, mandating them *to till and to keep* it. I notice dozens of farmworkers (*campesinos*) here, and I want to congratulate you for caring for the land, for cultivating it and for doing so in community. The elimination of so many brothers and sisters *campesinos* worries me, and it is not because of wars or natural disasters that they are uprooted. Land and water grabbing, deforestation, unsuitable pesticides are some of the evils which uproot people from their native land. This wretched separation is not only physical but existential and spiritual as well because there is a relationship with the land, such that rural communities and their special way of life are being put at flagrant risk of decline and even of extinction.

Francis then went on to talk about the issue of hunger: "The other dimension of this already global process is hunger. When financial speculation manipulates the price of food, treating it as just another commodity, millions of people suffer and die from hunger. At the same time, tons of food are thrown away. This constitutes a genuine scandal. Hunger is criminal, food is an inalienable right. I know that some of you are calling for agrarian reform in order to solve some of these problems, and let me tell you that in some countries—and here I cite *Compendium of the Social Doctrine of the Church*—'agrarian reform is, besides a political necessity, a moral obligation.'"

A second key point was *housing*. Francis called for "a home for every family."

> We must never forget that, because there was no room in the inn, Jesus was born in a stable; and that his family, persecuted by Herod, had to leave their home and flee into Egypt. Today there are so many homeless families, either because they have never had one or because, for different reasons, they have lost it. Family and housing go hand in hand. Furthermore, for a house to be a home, it requires a community dimension, and this is the neighbourhood . . . and it is precisely in the neighbourhood where the great family of humanity begins to be built, starting from the most immediate instance, from living together with one's neighbours. We live nowadays in immense cities that show off proudly, even arrogantly, how modern they are. But while they offer wellbeing and innumerable pleasures for a happy minority, housing is denied to thousands of our neighbours, our brothers and sisters including children, who are called elegant names such as "street people" or "without fixed abode" or "urban camper." Isn't it curious how euphemisms abound in the world of injustices! A person, a segregated person, a person set apart, a person who suffers misery or hunger: such a one is "urban camper." It is an elegant expression, isn't it? You should be on the lookout—I might be wrong in some cases; but in general, what lurks behind each euphemism is a crime.

The pope continued recalling what happens in big cities. "We live in cities that throw up skyscrapers and shopping centres and strike big real estate deals . . . but they abandon a part of themselves to marginal settlements on the periphery. How painful it is to hear that poor settlements are marginalized, or, worse still, earmarked for demolition! How cruel are the images of violent evictions, bulldozers knocking down the tiny dwellings, images just like from a war. And this is what we see today."

In contrast to this situation, the pope emphasized again that there is the experience of those neighborhoods where "values endure that have been forgotten in the rich centres," and where "public areas are not just transit corridors but an extension of the home, a place where bonds can be forged with neighbours. . . . How lovely are the cities that overcome unhealthy mistrust and integrate those who are different, even making such integration a new factor of development."

The third key point cited by Francis was *work*: "There is no worse material poverty—I really must stress this—there is no worse material poverty than the poverty which does not allow people to earn their bread, which deprives them of the dignity of work. But youth unemployment, informality or underground work, and the lack of labour rights are not inevitable. These are the result of an underlying social choice in favour of an economic system that puts profit above man. If economic profit takes precedence over the individual and over humanity, we find a throw-away culture at work that considers humanity in itself, human beings, as a consumer good, which can be used and then thrown away."

"This happens," said the pope, "when the deity of money is at the centre of an economic system rather than man, the human person. Yes, at the centre of every social or economic system must be the person, image of God, created to 'have dominion over' the universe. The inversion of values happens when the person is displaced and money becomes the deity."

Francis then commended all that the popular movements are doing: "Despite this throw-away culture, this culture of leftovers, so many of you who are excluded workers, the discards of this system, have been inventing your own work with materials that seemed to be devoid of further productive value. . . . But with the craftsmanship God gave you, with your inventiveness, your solidarity, your community work, your popular economy, you have managed to succeed, you are succeeding. . . . And let me tell you, besides work, this is poetry. I thank you."

"From now on, every worker," he added, "within the formal system of salaried employment or outside it, should have the right to decent remuneration, to social security and to a pension. Among you here are waste-collectors, recyclers, peddlers, seamstresses or tailors, artisans, fishermen, farmworkers, builders, miners, workers in previously abandoned enterprises, members of all kinds of cooperatives and workers in grassroots jobs who are excluded from labour rights, who are denied the possibility of unionizing, whose income is neither adequate nor stable. Today I want to join my voice to yours and support you in your struggle."

Finally, Francis spoke of peace in relation to ecology. "It is logical. There cannot be land, there cannot be housing, there cannot be work if we do not have peace and if we destroy the planet. These are such important topics that the peoples of the world and their popular organizations cannot fail to debate them. This cannot just remain in the hands of political leaders. All peoples of the earth, all men and women of good will—all of us must raise our voices in defence of these two precious gifts: peace and nature or 'Sister Mother Earth' as Saint Francis of Assisi called her."

"Recently I said and now I repeat, we are going through World War Three but in installments." Pope Francis mentioned again those "economic systems that must make war in order to survive," pointing out that "arms are manufactured and sold and, with that, the balance sheets of economies that sacrifice man at the feet of the idol of money are clearly rendered healthy."

"And no thought is given to hungry children in refugee camps; no thought is given to the forcibly displaced; no thought is given to destroyed homes; no thought is given, finally, to so many destroyed lives. How much suffering, how much destruction, how much grief. Today, dear brothers and sisters, in all parts of the earth, in all nations, in every heart and in grassroots movements, the cry wells up for peace: War no more!"

In the final part of his speech, Francis returned to talk about the integrity of creation:

An economic system centred on the deity money also needs to plunder nature to sustain consumption at the frenetic level it needs. Climate change, the loss of biodiversity, deforestation are already showing their devastating effects in terrible cataclysms which we see and from which you the humble suffer most—you who live near the coast in precarious dwellings, or so economically vulnerable that you lose everything due to a natural disaster. Brothers and sisters, creation is not a possession that we can dispose of as we wish; much less is it the property of some, of only a few. Creation is a gift, it is a present, it is a marvellous gift given to us by God so that we might care for it and use it, always gratefully and always respectfully, for the benefit of everyone. You may be aware that I am preparing an encyclical on ecology. Rest assured that your concerns will have their place in it.

"We talk about land, work, housing," said Francis. "We talk about working for peace and taking care of nature. Why are we accustomed to seeing decent work destroyed, countless families evicted, rural farmworkers driven off the land, war waged and nature abused? Because in this system man, the human person, has been removed from the centre and replaced by something else. Because idolatrous worship is devoted to money. Because indifference has been globalized: 'Why should I care what happens to others as long as I can defend what's mine?' Because the world has forgotten God, who is Father; and by setting God aside, it has made itself an orphan."

Pope Francis concluded by saying that "some of you said that this system cannot endure. We must change it. We must put human dignity back at the centre and on that pillar build the alternative social structures we need. This must be done with courage but also with intelligence, with tenacity but without fanaticism, with passion yet without violence. And all of us together, addressing the conflicts without getting trapped in them, always seeking to resolve the tensions in order to reach a higher plane of unity, of peace and of justice." Francis then said that Christians already have a guide to action, a "revolutionary" program: the Beatitudes in Matthew 5 and Luke 6 and the Last Judgment in Matthew 25.

"Moving towards a world of lasting peace and justice calls us to go beyond paternalistic forms of assistance; it calls us to create new forms of participation that include popular movements and invigorate local, national and international governing structures with that torrent of moral energy that springs from including the excluded in the building of a common destiny. And all this with a constructive spirit, without resentment, with love."

chapter 11

ECONOMIC SYSTEMS THAT MUST MAKE WAR IN ORDER TO SURVIVE

> *One can only note with dismay the evidence of a continuing growth in military expenditure and the flourishing arms trade, while the political and juridic process established by the international community for promoting disarmament is bogged down in general indifference. How can there ever be a future of peace when investments are still made in the production of arms and in research aimed at developing new ones?*

> —Benedict XVI, Message for the Celebration of the World Day of Peace 2006

Pope Francis's words and initiatives for peace and against war, especially in Syria, in the Gaza Strip, and in Iraq, are a topic that deserve a separate book. It suffices here to briefly remember some of the pope's interventions, highlighting how these may have contributed to alienate sympathy from those who hoped for his explicit "blessing" of the bombing of ISIS fundamentalists, the militants of the self-proclaimed Islamic caliphate that is moving its war of conquest in Iraq and in Syria, taking advantage of the instability that dominates the entire region.

In particular, it may be interesting to examine in this chapter those interventions in which Francis talked about the link between acts of war and the sale of weapons, between wars and the economy.

On Sunday, June 2, 2013, Pope Francis received in the Chapel of the *Domus Sanctae Marthae* thirteen soldiers injured during peacekeeping missions, most of whom had served in Afghanistan.[1] They were accompanied by their families and the relatives of twenty-four other soldiers killed during peacekeeping operations. Francis celebrated Mass for them, at the end of which the *Prayer for Italy*, composed by John Paul II, was recited.

During the homily, the pope said that war is "madness. It is the suicide of humanity. Because it kills the heart; it kills precisely that which is the Lord's message: it kills love! Because war comes from hatred, envy, desire for power, and—we have seen it many times—from that hunger for more power." Then Francis, referring to the "great of the earth" and the illusion of those who think of solving the "local problems and economic crises" through war, added: "Why? Because, for them, money is more important than people! And war is just that: an act of faith in money, in idols, in idols of hatred, in the idol that leads to killing one's brother, which leads to killing love."

Francis concluded: "It reminds me of the words of God our Father to Cain, who, out of envy, had killed his brother: 'Cain, where is your brother?' Today we can hear this voice: God our Father weeps, crying over this madness of ours, and who says to all of us: where is your brother? And to all who have power 'Where is your brother? What have you done?' . . . Behind a war there are always sins: the sin of idolatry, the sin of exploiting men on the altar of power, sacrificing them."

On September 8, 2013, the day after the Vigil of Prayer for Peace in Syria, which had registered significant participation from all over the world with people praying and fasting to avert a Western military intervention against Assad's regime—Francis pronounced unambiguous words against the arms trade and the traffickers of death. But he also reproached the powerful of the earth who are playing their military and commercial games at the expense of suffering civilians.

Francis's plea for peace was vibrant and heartfelt. To choose to do good "entails saying 'no' to the fratricidal hatred and falsehood that are used; saying 'no' to violence in all its forms; saying 'no' to the proliferation of weapons and to the illegal arms trade." These, warns Francis, are the enemies to fight, "united and consistent, following no other interests than those of peace and of the common good." The pope started from the gospel parable of the king going to war. A passage of Scripture that "at this moment in which we are praying intensely for peace, this word of the Lord touches us to the core."[2]

Francis then addressed the crowd returning to St. Peter's Square after the vigil of the previous day. Speaking more spontaneously, he pronounced these eloquent words: "And the doubt always remains: is this war or that war—because wars are everywhere—really a war to solve problems or is it a commercial war for selling weapons in illegal trade?"

The following day, Bishop Silvano Tomasi, permanent representative of the Holy See to the United Nations and other international organizations in Geneva, stated on Vatican Radio: "The proliferation of weapons continue to strengthen and nourish crime mafias of various types. Commercial interests—as the pope says—play an important role in arms transfer." Tomasi then recalled "the traffickers' profit and even the economic interests of states that produce and sell weapons, such as the United States, Russia, the UK, France, Germany, Israel, China, and others. These are states where the arms industry is a significant component of the economy." The market figures have been presented by SIPRI, the Stockholm International Peace Research Institute, which is dedicated to the monitoring of the international arms system: in the 2008–12 period there was a 17 percent increase in weapons exports in the world.

After the brief but intense pilgrimage to the Holy Land in May 2014, Pope Francis convened in Rome, at the Vatican, a meeting of "invocation for peace" between Israelis and Palestinians, inviting former President Shimon Peres and Palestinian President Abu Mazen. With them and the pope was also the ecumenical patriarch of Constantinople, Bartholomew. In the aftermath of that poignant moment, Francis gave an interview to journalist Henrique Cymerman, who had been involved in the preparation of the event. That interview was published in the Catalan newspaper *La Vanguardia* on June 12.

In one of his answers, the pope said:

> It's proven that with the food that is left over we could feed the people who are hungry. When you see photographs of undernourished kids in different parts of the world, you take your head in your hand, it is incomprehensible. I believe that we are in a world economic system that isn't good. At the center of all economic systems must be man, man and woman, and everything else must be in service of this man. But we have put money at the center, the god of money. We have fallen into a sin of idolatry, the idolatry of money.
>
> The economy is moved by the ambition of having more and, paradoxically, it feeds a throwaway culture. . . . But we are discarding an entire generation to maintain an economic system that can't hold up anymore, a system that to survive must make war, as the great empires have always done. But as a Third World War can't be done, they make zonal wars. What does this mean? That they produce and sell weapons, and with this the balance sheets of the idolatrous economies, the great world economies that sacrifice man at the feet of the idol of money, obviously they are sorted.[3]

A week after the publication of the interview, *The Economist* criticized Francis, comparing him to Lenin, and cast the interview as a "real bombshell." In particular, the English-language weekly newspaper targeted the pope's statements on the "idolatrous economies" feeding on wars.[4]

"By positing a link between capitalism and war," wrote *The Economist*, "[the pope] seems to be taking an ultra-radical line: one that consciously or unconsciously follows Vladimir Lenin in his diagnosis of capitalism and imperialism as the main reason why world war broke out a century ago. And there are plenty of counter-arguments one could offer. Many other ruling powers in history (from feudal warlords to secular totalitarian regimes) have had a more obvious stake in violence and confrontation than capitalism has. And thinkers like Joseph Schumpeter and Karl Popper have argued forcefully that capitalism can consolidate peace, by offering non-violent ways to satisfy human needs."

However, the same piece also recognized that on other points made during the interview Francis may have been right, even though he is not a "professor" like Benedict XVI. "But then, in contrast with his cerebral predecessor, Francis does not pretend either to be an academic philosopher, political scientist or economist; he is a more intuitive figure and his intuitions are often sound. He observes what he calls the 'idolatry of money' in some places and hungry children in others. He is viscerally distressed by the waste of human talent and energy among the young. He concludes that economists must be missing some important point. Francis may not be offering all the right answers, or getting the diagnosis exactly right, but he is asking the right questions. Like a little boy who observes the emperor's nakedness."

Francis also spoke strong and unambiguous words on the flight back from the trip to Korea in August 2014, in response to a question about the situation in Iraq and Islamic fundamentalist violence against religious minorities. The question was asked by Alan Holdren, an American journalist of the Catholic News Agency, ACI Prensa, and EWTN.

"Your Holiness, as you know, United States military forces have just begun to bomb terrorists in Iraq in order to prevent a genocide, to protect the future of minorities—I'm also thinking of the Catholics in your care. Do you approve of this American bombing?"[5]

Francis replied:

> In these cases, where there is an unjust aggression, I can only say that it is licit to stop the unjust aggressor. I emphasize the word: "stop." I'm not saying drop bombs, make war, but stop the aggressor. The means used to stop him would have to be evaluated. Stopping an unjust aggressor is licit. But we also need to remember! How many times, with this excuse of stopping an unjust aggressor, the powers have taken over peoples and carried on an actual war of conquest! One nation alone cannot determine how to stop an unjust aggressor. After the Second World War, there was the idea of the United Nations: that is where discussion was to take place, to say: "Is this an unjust aggressor? It would seem so. How do we stop him?" This alone, nothing else.

About minorities, the pope added: "Thanks for using that word. Because people say to me: 'the Christians, the poor Christians. . . .' And it is true, they are suffering, and martyrs, yes, there are many martyrs. But there are also men and women, religious minorities, not all Christians, and all are equal before God. To stop an unjust aggressor is a right of humanity, but it is also a right of the aggressor to be stopped in order not to do evil."

In response to another question, the pope said: "But turning to these instances of martyrdom and suffering, and these women: these are the fruits of war! Today we are in a world at war everywhere! Someone told me, 'You know, Father, we are in the Third World War, but it is being fought "piecemeal."' Do you understand? It is a world at war, where these acts of cruelty take place. I would like to reflect on two words. The first is cruelty. Today children don't count! We used to speak of conventional wars; today, this does not count. I'm not saying that conventional wars are a good thing, of course not. But today a bomb is dropped and kills the innocent with the guilty, the child and the woman with him, his mother. . . . They kill everybody. But we need to stop and think a bit about the degree of cruelty at which we have arrived. This should frighten us! I don't say this to create fear: one can make an empirical study. The degree of mankind's cruelty is presently frightening."

With his answer on the American bombing in Iraq, Pope Francis refused to join those who in the West seem to want to present what is happening as a clash of civilizations between Islam and Christianity—which is precisely what the fundamentalists want. While recognizing the right and the duty to stop the aggressor and, therefore, to intervene forcefully to stop genocide and massacres, Francis does not endorse operations that turn into wars of conquest intended to "take over" peoples. He insists on the role of an institution that seems almost forgotten and is no longer mentioned when dealing with international crises: the United Nations. Francis is realistic about the situation in the Middle East, devastated by conflicts fought in the name of an "exportable" democracy that resulted only in destabilization and chaos.

One can imagine that the pope's unambiguous words on the arms trade, wars made to sell weapons, and idolatrous economies that feed on conflicts, as well as his distancing from those who would have liked to see him more compliant with the Western bombing operations, did not help him make many friends in certain and well-known circles.

Pope Francis returned to the war and its folly on September 13, 2014, during the Mass celebrated at the Military Memorial of Redipuglia, Italy, on the occasion of the centennial of the outbreak of the First World War.

"After experiencing the beauty of traveling throughout this region, where men and women work and raise their families, where children play and the elderly dream . . . I now find myself here, in this place, near this cemetery, able to say only one thing: War is madness."[6]

"Whereas God carries forward the work of creation," continued Francis,

> and we men and women are called to participate in his work, war destroys. It also ruins the most beautiful work of his hands: human beings. War ruins everything, even the bonds between brothers. War is irrational; its only plan is to bring destruction: it seeks to grow by destroying. Greed, intolerance, the lust for power. . . . These motives underlie the decision to go to war, and they are too often justified by an ideology; but first there is a distorted passion or impulse. Ideology is presented as a justification and when there is no ideology, there is the response of Cain: "What does it matter to me? Am I my brother's keeper?" War does not look directly at anyone, be they elderly, children, mothers, fathers. . . . "What does it matter to me?"

Francis then returned to the idea of a third world war "fought piecemeal, with crimes, massacres, destruction. . . . In all honesty, the front page of newspapers ought to carry the headline, 'What does it matter to me?'" This attitude, said Francis, "is the exact opposite of what Jesus asks of us in the Gospel. We have heard: he is the least of his brothers; he, the King, the Judge of the world, he is the one who hungers, who thirsts, he is the stranger, the one who is sick, the prisoner.

"Here and in other cemeteries," continued Francis, "lie many victims. Today, we remember them. There are tears, there is mourning, there is sadness. From this place we remember the victims of every war. Today, too, the victims are many. . . . How is this possible? It is so because in today's world, behind the scenes, there are interests, geopolitical strategies, lust for money and power, and there is the manufacture and sale of arms, which seem to be so important! And these plotters of terrorism, these schemers of conflicts, just like arms dealers, have engraved in their hearts, 'What does it matter to me?'"

"It is the task of the wise," explained Francis, "to recognize errors, to feel pain, to repent, to beg for pardon and to cry. With this 'What does it matter to me?' in their hearts, the merchants of war have perhaps made a great deal of money, but their corrupted hearts have lost the capacity to cry. Cain did not cry. He was not capable of tears. The shadow of Cain hangs over us today in this cemetery. It has been seen here. It is seen from 1914 right up to our own time. It is seen even in the present."

"With the heart of a son, a brother, a father," concluded Francis, "I ask each of you, indeed for all of us, to have a conversion of heart: to move on from 'What does it matter to me?' to tears: for each one of the fallen of this 'senseless massacre,' for all the victims of the mindless wars, in every age. Weeping. Brothers and sisters, humanity needs to weep, and this is the time to weep."

chapter 12

SOCIAL DOCTRINE IN A WORLD GOVERNED BY FINANCIAL TECHNOCRATS

The teaching of Leo XIII, so noble and lofty and so utterly new to worldly ears, was held suspect by some, even among Catholics, and to certain ones it even gave offense. For it boldly attacked and overturned the idols of Liberalism, ignored long-standing prejudices, and was in advance of its time beyond all expectation.

—Pius XI, *Quadragesimo Anno*

In order to continue on our path of investigation on the effects of Pope Francis's inteventions and more generally of those—largely forgotten—of his predecessors, we met with two personalities of the Catholic world who in various capacities deal with financial-economic issues, and we asked them how they respond to the pope's messages. Their points of view are obviously different due to their different education, profession, and sensitivity. Both have worked, however, albeit in different positions, for the Holy See.

Our first conversation is with Ettore Gotti Tedeschi, who for three years chaired the Institute for the Works of Religion (IOR), where he had been called by Benedict XVI to develop the IOR's objective of transparency and bring it in line with international anti-money laundering laws. Born in March 1945, one month before the end of the war, to a displaced family in a farmhouse in

Pontenure, Italy, a village a few kilometers from Piacenza, Gotti led the IOR from September 2009 to May 2012.

Since 1993 he has been the president of the Italian branch of Banco Santander. He was president of the Fund for Infrastructure promoted by the Italian government, as well as director of the Loan and Savings Fund and economic adviser to the minister of economy and finances Giulio Tremonti. He worked for the first thirteen years of his career in strategic consulting, in Paris at Semae, and in Italy and the UK at McKinsey. Then he entered the world of finance, assuming the position of head of the merchant banking group IMI, and later cofounded Akros Financial, after which he brought Banco Santander to Italy. Until December 2006, he was director and a member of the executive committee of the Bank Sanpaolo of Turin. His most recent book is *Amare Dio e fare soldi. Massime di economia divina* (To Love God and Make Money. Principles of Divine Economy).[1]

Do you share the alarm raised by Pope Francis in the apostolic exhortation Evangelii Gaudium *on the economy that "kills"?*

How could I not? The pope is showing the way to overcome the inequalities, precariousness, and undignified conditions of the human being. He says no to an economy of exclusion, an economy that leads humanity to ignore their neighbors, to be selfish and indifferent, which instead of leading to solidarity and love leads to loneliness. A misuse of the economic instrument can be considered a real "sin," but in order to fight and overcome it we must first overcome the "moral poverty" that leads humanity to embrace "an economy that kills." If we start from the assumption that the economy is only an essentially neutral means, then it becomes clear that those who use it are the same ones who give it a meaning, a direction, leading it toward specific views. Clearly it is not the economy that kills, but it is a specific use of it as a means that has negative consequences. Therefore, equitable and just economic models may be proposed and implemented only if those at the helm consider them the means to achieve the common good and, above all, they must be willing to do so. Who needs to be changed and educated in these terms is humanity. A guiding perspective, in this case, has to be the social doctrine of the church rather than the regulatory state; but in this gnostic and nihilistic world that body of teaching struggles to be accepted. The problem is that the economic model currently used, which I call empirical global capitalism, was conceived on neo-Malthusian assumptions, such as "not having children is good for the economy and civilization." These ideas have led to harmful results that are detrimental even to humanity and its economic development; they have "killed" the will to procreate and have become the underlying cause for an increasing difficulty in caring for the aging population. The current economic model has been specifically designed to compensate for the lack of development due to the sharp decline in birth rates in the Western world, and was founded on the growth of individual consumerism, which is increasingly based on credit. To support this illusory growth we have created growing imbalances: we have sacrificed our savings in favor of consumption; we have accelerated the aging of populations, resulting in fixed costs that, in order to be absorbed, drive up taxes to untenable levels. And then other imbalances were created by deindustrialization that have resulted in unemployment and the loss of purchasing power. Finally, additional imbalances were created by the decision to relocate industrial production in other countries where the cost of labor is very low in order to increase the purchasing power with cheaper goods that were imported to replace those produced within the country. But this pattern of relocation has also allowed rapid industrialization of entire economic areas that have gained access to material well-being, thus denying doomsday predictions made years earlier by the same neo-Malthusians. Of course, we should reflect first on what "well-being" really means. According to gnostic pragmatism, it is the only thing capable of producing tangible, material results. Whereas for Catholic culture it is a balanced synthesis of three fulfillments: the material, the intellectual, and the spiritual, since we are made of body, mind, and soul. Nihilistically eliminating the other two, material satisfaction alone commodifies human life, and puts at risk the real integral progress for humanity, for which Paul VI called in *Populorum Progressio*. This commodification of life "fills bellies and hearts, " but is followed by debts, taxes, and risks that are impossible to predict. This system has only temporarily, and only superficially, eased working and existential conditions. So, in conclusion, I fully share the pope's alarm; an alarm that was already launched by Benedict XVI in the introduction to *Caritas in Veritate*, in which he explained how the dominant gnostic and nihilistic culture has left total moral autonomy to the economic instrument. The economic instrument, in turn, has followed the pragmatic truth that has no end in itself and that specifically turns economic means into ends, thus derailing everything and for which even human beings become means.

Francis has criticized "trickle-down" economic theories and for that reason he was attacked and called a Marxist. Do you agree with these allegations against the pope? Is the pope right or not?

History reminds us of how many utopias have deluded and confused humanity over the centuries, even though it is undeniable that "trickle-down" policies, under certain circumstances, have effectively worked. But if we think about it more closely, these circumstances are all related to the observance of natural laws in economics; when these are ignored, there is no trickle-down effect, or it's only illusory. Gnosticism has always dreamed of being able to recreate a new world with new and always better laws to correct the "wrong" nature of the imagined creation. This form of gnosis is based on the knowledge of human beings and wants to convince them that perfection is achievable in this world thanks to the path opened by idealistic scientists and technocrats. Great men ended up "deluding" themselves: St. Thomas More in his work *Utopia* imagined to create a world without private property; Hobbes in *Leviathan* thought of setting man free from original sin. If you think about it, even Adam Smith's position on the trickle-down effect is a consequence of his supposed faith in the invisible hand of the free and autonomous market, and he himself, knowing the rules of the market, realized that it was a utopian theory. But if Smith himself did not really believe in it, if the world is often governed by utopias that prove to be unattainable, if we recognize that economics is not a science, why then should we be surprised when the pope says that a particular economic theory, unproven and empiricist as it is, has been used in certain circumstances to deceive the weak and the less self-sufficient? If we look at what has happened over the last thirty years, we can see that trickle-down effects have occurred in Asia thanks to the relocation industry. However, in the Western world there has been an endless series of economic and social "trickle-down side effects," due to wrong moral-economic-political decisions. Think about the illusion of greater prosperity stemming from lower birth rates and the consequent side effects such as an aging population and the need to care for the elderly, tax increases, debt, and the destruction of savings; think of the fallout resulting from decisions taken on the basis of television educational and cultural models so as to stimulate the consumer attitude. Supporters of trickle-down theories should not dwell only on theory, but on reality. It is obvious, or desirable, that those who take decisions on economic policy want to generate greater prosperity using trickle-down theories; but we must look at the facts and accept that these have been harmful. This does not mean that capitalist economy is wrong, but that capitalism is contradictory; it produces material wealth but it confuses means and ends. John Paul II had foreseen it in *Sollicitudo Rei Socialis*; Benedict XVI explained its logic and motives in *Caritas in Veritate*; and in *Lumen Fidei* Francis focused on the spiritual solutions. Economic theories and laws must be consistent with natural laws—that is, those of creation. And the pope is by definition the best "economist" in this sense, because he knows the logic of creation, the logic of the resulting natural laws, and he knows better than anyone else humanity and its economic, intellectual, and spiritual needs.

Is the most recent form of capitalism, the one in which we are living today, a somewhat irreversible system?

Those who in the past believed that the crisis of capitalism was irreversible were the ones who thought that the exploited and organized masses were tearing it down. I fear that those who declare today that this crisis is irreversible are those who are planning its transformation in order to continue to control it without arousing suspicion. However, capitalism has already gone through several transformations, even radical ones, throughout history: it originated in a Catholic environment but got "corrupted" in a Protestant one; it was distorted by the Enlightenment, which changed it from a means to an end, and altered by Marxism; and then it was transformed once again with the advent of utilitarianism and technocracy that created new technocratic high priests ready to change it in global capitalism. At this point, however, what John Paul II predicted in *Sollicitudo Rei Socialis* about capitalism has occurred: humanity is "not ready" to handle sophisticated instruments and these have gotten out of hand. Globally, where there are collisions between cultures, civilizations, ethical systems with different views on what is good and beautiful, and how to achieve them, the traits of capitalism are relativized. Allow me to explain: current capitalism is of the gnostic type that, perhaps without realizing it, aims to make people happy and fulfilled, but only from a materialistic point of view. It would be interesting to know what the fatalist Hindus, the Chinese Taoists-Buddhists, or Muslims think about that. Even in our civilization, which, despite experiencing a strong moral decline, we recognize to be founded on Christian roots, there is the problem of what position to take toward this form of capitalism that does not take into account ethics and culture. The point here is that those who corrupt capitalism as we know it today, are also ready to modify it according to opportunities and needs, and to transform and adjust it, as long as it remains the same system of power.

Can a more ethical economic system—led by men and women who care about the common good—bring about change and a greater focus on social justice and the redistribution of wealth, or is it also right to hypothesize a restructuring of the system?

But how do you put more ethics in the economy? Imposing it by some Quranic law? Proposing it and then convincing others of its usefulness? And would we be able to achieve structural changes in the system to ensure more ethics? To begin, we should ask: What produces social injustice, selfishness in the distribution of wealth, and, accordingly, what produces solidarity, and so on? As a Catholic, I believe it is a priority to solve the problem of "moral poverty" before the problems of poverty and economic justice. I believe it is the predisposition to sin, envy, corruption, arrogance that induces humanity to reject solidarity. Only "mature" human beings, who have gone through a process of acquiring knowledge, are able to attain detachment from goods and possessions. Popes have been teaching these things for hundreds of years, but few listen to them. Keep in mind that once the "enemies" were Marxism and liberalism, both the product of gnosticism. Today, instead, we have nihilism and relativism that claim moral autonomy for the economy and promise well-being and irrelevant, unattainable healthy goals and material satisfactions. These forces give rise to a new form of theological relativism and are preparing the ground for a new faith and spirituality that is essentially naturalistic and pantheistic, while maintaining environmentalism as a common belief and bringing together the entire world in a shared ideal, in order to eliminate the mediation of the social teaching of the church. The church has always taught what is the correct economic order, according to the Truth; it also teaches how to live the virtues that sanctify the economy, thus sanctifying the same economic operators and those who indirectly benefit from this system. A fair and moral economy can exist only if humanity can give meaning to the use of the economic instrument, and this can happen only when it regains the meaning of life. It makes no sense to search for new instruments, new structures; we must accompany humanity along a path. If the instruments are managed by the same humanity, with the same intent, they end up producing the same results.

How important is it for Christians to recover a sense of the protection of creation and sustainable development?

As I said previously, the risk is that we end up confusing faith in God and respect for the environment. The respect for creation is a duty of the creature toward its Creator; this respect implies significant investments in technology, so we have to think about what is sustainable development. Catholic ethics of environmental concern are consistent with the Truth and have nothing to do with naturalistic, pantheistic, pagan cults; it does not follow the globalized model of the New Age. Humanity, however, has the responsibility to use and protect the environment, as a gift of God and for its own good.

Why does a certain part of the U.S. neoconservative world struggle to understand Pope Francis?

I'm unable to offer a complete and correct assessment of this matter. I have read a few comments; they seem to me dictated by the urge to be at the center of attention, a lack of humility, a certain way of doing, typical of the competitive American Catholic Puritanism, rather than by the desire to help improve Catholic thinking on certain issues. Besides, the specific contradiction of capitalism that gave rise to the current crisis started in the United States, not in Rome; but I do not remember reading heartfelt warnings sent by neoconservatives to the U.S. government. In some cases, however, we must try not to analyze and judge superficially, and we must look instead at the context: Michael Novak, for example, wants to defend Catholic thought in the face of certain philo-Protestant circles always arguing that Catholicism is the cause of the economic slowdown, and he is concerned that some of the pope's positions can give them new fodder for similar allegations.

Why do Pius XI's strong and prophetic words, in his encyclical Quadragesimo Anno, *against the international imperialism of money sound so radical and extreme that not even the most leftist politician would ever dream of using them today?*

I think there are many reasons for that. First of all, today it is customary to use and hear politically correct, and never unpopular, statements. Then, probably, they want to avoid the parallels between the current crisis and that of 1929—the same crisis whose causes and effects were mentioned and discussed by Pope Pius XI in *Quadragesimo Anno*. Perhaps today there are no more true leftist politicians; also, let us not forget that *Quadragesimo Anno* arrived forty years after Leo XIII's *Rerum Novarum*, if we really want to observe and assess the disasters of liberal economy. I also believe that, after eighty years since 1931, today's nihilist culture tries to avoid giving due attention to moral references no longer considered relevant. In those days, the pope's strong words were accepted, but now they irritate even the Catholic world. Pius XI's criticism was directed toward the "authoritative capitalism" as practiced by financial holding companies influenced by politics and leaning toward monopolistic powers characterized by the concentration of wealth and rejection of the competitive market. I would even characterize this as Malthusian capitalism, which was in the hands of those who laid down the laws of the market in order to impose a criterion of survival, which excluded the weak and the law-abiding, while, in fact, it controlled the economy with every means available, including those of political influence. Pius XI's words were prophetic in that he sensed that this form of capitalism would not allow a fair distribution of wealth, but rather, more than with the capitalism projected by various liberal economic schools, seemed to compete with the totalitarian system implemented a little later in communist countries, where it was concentrated in the hands of the state without a capitalist, private bourgeois class. Pius XI launched a proposal: a new Christian order based on the subsidiarity of the state to individuals, as well as a form of solidaristic individualism. He proposed that same new order that inspired Luigi Einaudi's assessment in defining the social doctrine of the church as the "third way" beyond capitalism and socialism, a path that combined individual freedom and solidarity. All these considerations and proposals, however, presupposed moral reflections on the meaning of life and our actions, and this clashed with the foolish and reckless haste with which in those days they were seeking a solution to the ongoing crisis. Another obstacle was, and still is, ideological. If Catholics act, they act to change the world; this world, however, should not be changed by Catholic morality. Perhaps the pope's considerations are ignored in favor of others considered more appropriate for this world, which exerts a certain kind of power and wants the encouragement and support of the world's highest moral authority and not his reproach.

Why are these themes, which belong to the teaching and doctrine of the church, so overlooked despite the fact that they photographed very clearly a situation similar to the one we find ourselves in today, eighty years after Pius XI's encyclical?

For the reasons I have just mentioned. Because we are experiencing a progression and metamorphosis of the spiritual knowledge that would like to "fix" creation precisely with the help of the church, trying to get her to rewrite the Bible. Knowing, very superficially and without understanding it clearly, the essence of the expression *non prevalebunt* (they shall not prevail).

Do you think that much can be done with a new leadership and the commitment of laypeople who have the confidence to take risks on these issues, even daring to question the system in which we live?

I do think so. By the way, this was advocated by Pius XI himself in the encyclical mentioned above, in which the pope invited the laity, engaged in the economic sector, to act in an apostolic manner wherever they found themselves. But the difficulties are many. First, a part of the laity does not seem to be willing to work with the necessary spirit of service, in total commitment, but rather tends to mask its aspiration for personal power with statements of service to the church. Second, the laity that could take on this leadership role collides with the "duties" and "values" that the world wants to impose. Further, the laity encounters difficulties in relations with that part of the church that should support and encourage it—namely, with that form of clericalism that damages the church. Too often what is lacking is either the integrity of the laity, or the support to their actions. History confirms that the commitment of the laity is only, or particularly, successful if it is properly supported by the ecclesiastical structure; only the church can give credibility to the laity's actions. Unfortunately, what happens is that when a part of the church decides to support certain projects, another may decide to ignore them. If we look back to the commitment of the laity in contemporary history, however, we find a few exceptional cases, such as Giuseppe Toniolo or Giuseppe Antonio Tovini, who achieved extraordinary results (and, in fact, the church has declared them blessed and "candidates to holiness").

Are the paragraphs of Populorum Progressio, *stating that private property is not an absolute right but is subject to the common good, and the claims of the* Catechism of Saint Pius X, *according to which the sins that cry to heaven for vengeance are the oppression of the poor and defrauding workers of their just wages, still valid today?*

Populorum Progressio is an extraordinary encyclical that I provocatively call "utopian." It addresses the question, which I mentioned before, of the three fulfillments of humanity: the material-economic, the intellectual–cultural, and the spiritual. The economic alone turns a human being into a materialistic and consumeristic animal, while the material along with the intellectual create a pragmatic and rational one. Spiritual satisfaction alone turns a person into an ascetic; if we add the material to the spiritual we have a sentimental who is unable to rationally explain the reason for his actions. The spiritual and intellectual together, however, can potentially create a blessed person. These three fulfillments should be in harmony with each other, but more often than not they are in conflict. Generally, whoever provides material satisfaction manages the intellectual and tends to downplay the spiritual. The key point of that encyclical is the relationship between people and things. Paul VI, fascinated by the thought of the great contemporary intellectual Jean Guitton—who wrote that "a man really possesses only what he can do without, and it is clear that if a man cannot do without something then that something possesses him"—held that the detachment from goods and assets was the true test of the maturity of a lived, charitable Christianity and proof of its true freedom. While I share Paul VI's views, I also believe that the right to private property cannot be exercised against the common good; if it were so, we would affirm the moral principle that the common good is greater than the individual. I do not know if the pope was referring to abuses in the use of private property, but it is clear that for him the detachment from goods was something essential to salvation and solidarity. Material satisfaction, in fact, is just one of the fulfillments we should achieve; the magisterium of the church is full of references to "the things above" instead of the ones down here on earth: the life of a person "does not consist of possessions" (Luke 12:15). While we live on earth, however, we have to consider that the "means" are necessary, as is private property, which allows greater protection and guarantees of individual freedom. The common good is not realized by transforming private property into collective property, but through solidarity, with the awareness that nothing that is ours is truly our own, but it has been given to us, and we should put it to good use. The common good is realized with a form of caring and loving solidaristic individualism, as the one outlined by the social doctrine of the church that is the basis of a Catholic capitalism capable of reconciling freedom and solidarity.

We come now to the second point of your question. Over the last thirty years, to support an economic growth of the consumerist type and to remedy the lack of growth of the GDP, the industrialized, rich, expensive, welfare-prone Western countries, where workers were paid a fair wage, had to lower the price of goods to increase the purchasing power of the people and thus reactivate the market. This led to the relocation of production in countries not yet industrialized, where a different criterion to determine the cost of production and fair wages was created. What is a fair wage? Is it what I can pay in another country to manufacture the same product that I produce at home and remain competitive on the market? Or is it the unionized pay rates that I would have to pay for the type of factory I own to allow my workers to live with dignity according to the local purchasing power? The answer is complex. We may look at it with a bit of irony and ask which came first, the chicken or the egg. In our case it would be: did the cost of competition between countries come first and then the need to choose where to produce, or was this type of competition created by exporting production? The correct answer is the second; but was it a good or a bad thing? It's definitely been good for the countries where production was transferred and where the economic well-being had been exported, but it has been bad for us to just relocate production in order to consume more at a lower cost without producing or revitalizing the economic activities. In practical terms, we have created, unconsciously, a temporary and opportunistic redistribution of wealth on a global scale. This, however, was not accomplished out of Christian love toward these countries; we did it in order to consume more. And we consumed more not because it was necessary, but to prevent the collapse of the GDP, which in turn was caused by the sharp decline in birth rates that we talked about earlier. In fact, the GDP can grow only through individual consumption. This, however, is not enough. If the population is not growing it means that it is getting older; and if aging decreases the number of those who produce, it increases the number of those who must be cared for; thus, we have increased health and welfare spending. This can be absorbed only through taxes, which grow in proportion and affect both consumption and investments. Therefore, to grow the GDP we consume on credit, but when the credit is not paid back everything collapses. The cause of all this is not to be found in the greed of bankers, however, but among the political leaders and the neo-Malthusians who have decided that the world had to have fewer inhabitants. From there derives the financial capitalism that now concerns us so much. At the beginning of it all, however, there is original sin, as highlighted by Paul VI in *Humanae Vitae*.

In today's globalized society, what are the possible applications and implications of teachings that are not only social but are at the very heart of the Christian faith?

If I wanted to be provocative, I could say that in today's globalized society we may even get to the point of forbidding the teachings of the Christian faith. My fear is that if Catholicism is unable to "convert" the whole world it will be forced to adapt to the world, thus relativizing its faith. There is however a third option: be prepared for new persecutions and from these draw the strength to convert the world. The Catholic faith is absolutist in its truths, in its dogmas; not only does it explain the meaning of life, it also tells us how to behave and asks us to realize its works. Catholics have "duties" toward their Creator. They cannot separate faith from works; otherwise they break the unity of life and contradict their own faith. Faith must inspire works—not vice versa. If works inspire faith it means that these are influenced by the world and are based on the morality of the dominant culture. In our global world, faith and works confront each other within different religious ethics (monotheistic or parareligious) and with several and more various secular ethics, often all incompatible in the choice of the truth, or the freedom, that should inspire behavior. What I fear is that the world will force Catholicism to become mere practical social ethics, with the risk of becoming a caricature of the Catholicism lived by the saints. What we should reflect on is that the application of Catholic doctrine, by its nature, would change the world if it were really lived, and this is what the world has always feared and fought. A Catholicism that is not lived is useless; it does not sanctify the person or society, nor does it affect the world. But if the Catholic world were to reaffirm its foundations of faith, for many reasons it would be accused of being a liability for the world: because it tyrannizes humanity with the sense of sin, or because it dictates a "fundamentalist and intransigent" faith, thus creating discord and hindering the cultural homogenization of the world. Whereas, in exchange for the willingness to relativize our faith, many are the suggested advantages: to be appreciated and co-opted by the world and the overcoming of fatigue, pain, suffering, thanks to science and technology. Let me conclude by saying that we should be surprised that Catholics are unable to have the more secular world appreciate the fruits of its doctrine. In recent history, many of the more secular intellectuals have recognized the importance of the works of faith. Consider Murray Rothbard, a Jewish-American liberal economist who wrote that "all that is good in Western civilization is due to Christianity"; or Friedrich von Hayek, the Austrian economist, an exponent of liberalism, who said that "the best teachings for our culture are the ones derived from Christianity"; and Lew Rockwell, the American economist and the greatest exponent of the Austrian school, who said that "Christianity gave birth to compassionate individualism that made possible the development of capitalism." Therefore, we must have the courage to still deserve these appreciations. Pope Francis's first encyclical, *Lumen Fidei*, explains what kind of support the church must offer to the faithful in order to achieve that.

Can the world dominated by finance still be called capitalism? And what relationship does it have, or not have, with the real economy?

I don't think so. Finance took over when, say, in the 1980s, savings were reduced and debt began to grow. More debt and less savings have made finance the primary resource, and the "banker-financier" has become the new technocratic high priest. In practical terms, finance takes over when we ignore and mess with the natural laws that must guide the real economic laws. When we ignore the teachings and recommendations of *Humanae Vitae* and *Populorum Progressio*, what is left? It is obvious that it can no longer be called capitalism since the expression "financial capitalism" is in itself incorrect. A world dominated by finance is an illusory world dominated by an unsustainable and unnatural consumerism founded on the belief that humanity should be fulfilled in a materialistic manner. As I have already said, to rebuild a world that appreciates a capitalism founded on the real economy, we must start from the social doctrine of the church. Why has it never been put into practice? Because in order to do so we must have faith—and the world today has none.

chapter 13

CAPITALIST ECONOMY AND CIVIL MARKET ECONOMY

> *The richer class have many ways of shielding themselves, and stand less in need of help from the State; whereas the mass of the poor have no resources of their own to fall back upon, and must chiefly depend upon the assistance of the State.*
>
> —Leo XIII, *Rerum Novarum*

Our second contribution on the issues raised by *Evangelii Gaudium*—and on the forgetfulness that sometimes seems to exist in the Catholic world regarding some relevant and surprising pages of the social doctrine of the church—is a dialogue with Professor Stefano Zamagni. Born in 1943 in Rimini, Italy, Zamagni is professor of political economy at the University of Bologna's faculty of economics and adjunct professor of international political economy at Johns Hopkins University. He graduated in 1966 in economics from the Catholic University of the Sacro Cuore in Milan, and, from 1969 to 1973, he specialized at the University of Oxford, at Linacre College. Before Bologna, he taught at the University of Parma and, until 2007, at the Bocconi University in Milan as a professor of the history of economic analysis. From 2007 to 2012, Zamagni was president of the Italian Commission for the Non-Profit Sector. In 2010, he was awarded the Georgio La Pira prize for peace. In 2013, he was awarded the first Economy and Society international award of the foundation Centesimus

Annus. Also in 2013, the Foundation of Subiaco awarded him the Saint Benedict European Prize. He is a member of the scientific committee of several national and international economic journals and of the Pontifical Academy of Social Sciences. He is the author of numerous scientific publications and other contributions to cultural and scientific debate. His most recent books are *Famiglia e lavoro* (Family and Work) and *Impresa responsabile e mercato civile* (Responsible Business Enterprise and the Civil Market).[1]

Do you share the alarm raised by Pope Francis in the apostolic exhortation Evangelii Gaudium *on the economy that kills?*

What Pope Francis launched in *Evangelii Gaudium* is not a warning, but a heartfelt invitation to reconsider the foundations of the model of market economy now in vogue. It is therefore an invitation to leave behind the "night of thought" in which this crisis forces us to dwell. Markets are not all equal, because they are the "precipitate" of cultural and political projects. There is a market that reduces inequality and one that increases it. The first is called civil, because it broadens the *civitas* as it aims to include virtually all; the second is the uncivilized market, because it tends to exclude and restore the "existential suburbs." In the current phase of financial capitalism, the second type of market has become dominant, and the results are before our eyes: an increase of social inequalities to a level never seen in previous centuries and a decline of fundamental, and not symbolic, freedoms for too many people. It is to this situation, and not to a hypothetical reality, that the pope draws the attention of all, believers and nonbelievers. The fact is that the pope's words have a solid theoretical foundation much more than what a certain official media version wants people to believe. His approach is that of historical realism: reconnect knowledge and experience of reality and turn thought into life practice. Therefore, for Pope Francis, Christianity cannot be reduced to one orthodoxy, the risk of rationalistic intellectualism, nor to one orthopraxis—that is, a kind of spiritual pathos. What this means in concrete terms is that in addition to the *factum*—that is, what humanity does—there is the *faciendum*—that is, what it *can do* for a new historical project.

Francis has criticized the "trickle-down" economic theories and for this he was attacked and called a Marxist. Do you agree with these allegations against the pope? Is the pope right or not?

The theory known in economic literature as "trickle-down economics," effectively rendered the aphorism—first used, it seems, by the American economist Alan Blinder—that "a rising tide lifts all boats." For a long time, advocates of neoliberalism believed in it; there was no need to be concerned about the distribution of income and wealth because eventually everyone will see improvements. The important relevant thing was to increase the size of the pie (the GDP) without worrying about the size of the individual portions. It is on this that the well-known conservative adage is founded: "We do not need to care for the poor because each new rich is one less poor." Well, the pope tells us that in the current historical conditions (market globalization and financialization of the economy) the "trickle-down" effect can no longer happen, as any economist not blinded by preconceived notions well knows: the famous "Kuznets curve" is no longer valid today. Thus, the pope is right from a scientific perspective; so much so that the criticisms that have been made are only ideological (the pope has become a Marxist!). The truth is that Francis proves that he understands what too many observers and scholars pretend not to see—namely, that poverty, absolute poverty, and inequality are substantially different phenomena. Therefore, they also require different control strategies: if the fight against absolute poverty requires interventions on redistributive mechanisms, progress on the second front requires action at the very moment in which wealth is produced. And this bothers many!

Is the most recent form of capitalism, the one we are living today, a somewhat irreversible system?

Capitalism is one, but the varieties of capitalism are many. And the varieties change in relation to both cultural matrices prevalent in the societies in which they are applied and the characteristics of the historical period taken into consideration. There is

nothing irreversible in capitalism, as well as in other socioeconomic systems. Another important point to keep in mind is the
distinction between market economy and capitalist economy.
The first anticipates at least a couple of centuries the advent of
the second. This explains why markets are not all equal. For example, the civil economy market—a term first coined by Antonio
Genovesi in 1753—does not accept what Joseph Schumpeter in
1912 called the engine of capitalism—namely, what he called
"creative destruction." The capitalist market must "destroy"—
that is, expel businesses and people who are unproductive or
even just less productive—in order to create what is new and
thus expand indefinitely. This version of social Darwinism ends
up reducing economic relations between people to relationships
between things and these to goods. According to the pope, this
model of capitalism, typical of the current historical phase, is no
longer sustainable.

*Why does a part of the American neoconservative world struggle to
understand Pope Francis?*

There may be many reasons for the flat rejection of the pope's
message within a certain neoconservative world. A first reason
could be the fear that the pope intends to spend himself in favor
of pauperism and condemn wealth in itself, which is unfounded.
In his 2014 Lenten message, the pope clarified the difference
between poverty as evangelical virtue and extreme poverty. Extreme poverty is the lack of what is essential to life, with no hope
or solution in sight. Evangelical poverty is the detachment from
goods and possessions in view of a greater freedom. What Francis
is trying to emphasize are the ways in which wealth is generated
and the criteria by which it is distributed among the members of
the human family; not being purely of a technical order, a Christian cannot but submit to moral judgment these ways and criteria.
A second reason is that a certain conservatism is concerned about
the lack of support on the part of the social doctrine of the church
for a particular model of market economy. But Christianity, as a
universalist and nonethnic religion, can never be incorporated

in a particular system of social order, a system that relies on a particular and historically determined cultural matrix. These concerns, as understandable as they may be, are not however justifiable within a Christian theological perspective.

Why do Pius XI's strong and prophetic words in his encyclical Quadragesimo Anno, *against the international imperialism of money, sound so radical and extreme that not even the most leftist politician would ever dream of using them today?*

Pius XI's words in *Quadragesimo Anno* should be read against the background of what was happening then. The crisis of 1929 was the first major crisis of capitalism and it also, like the present one, originated in the financial sector. Consider the current situation. As Marco Vitale informs us, in 1980 the global financial assets were equal to the world GDP ($27 trillion). In 2007, on the eve of the outbreak of the crisis, it had increased to $240 trillion against the $60 trillion of the world's GDP—four times more. And at present that gap has become even larger. Over that same period of time, in most countries the wage share relative to the GDP fell by more than nine points, resulting in an increase of the financial income share. When facing such phenomena, I don't think that expressions such as "international imperialism of money" sound too exaggerated!"

Why are these themes, which belong to the teaching and doctrine of the church, so overlooked despite the fact that they photographed very clearly a situation similar to the one we find ourselves in today, eighty years after Pius XI's encyclical?

The answer to this question requires a clarification that, to my knowledge, is never provided. In October 1829, the famous professor of economics at the University of Oxford, Richard Whately, was the first to formulate the principle of NOMA (*Non-Overlapping Magisteria*)—that is, if the economy is to become a science, it must be separated from ethics and politics. Why? The answer is simple: politics is the realm of the ends that society pursues; ethics is the realm of the values that should guide human behavior; and the economy is the realm of the most effective means to achieve those ends with regard to those values. Thus the economy does not need to "go haywire" with the other two spheres. All the subsequent economic thought—with few exceptions—has accepted the principle of NOMA and with good reason, as can be easily understood. Since the advent of globalization in the late 1970s, we have gradually witnessed a radical reversal of roles: the economy becomes the realm of ends, and politics that of means. This is the reason why, as all observers have not failed to notice, democracy today is at the service of the market. The influential and powerful president of the Bundesbank, Hans Tietmeyer, understood it ahead of his time, when in 1996 he stated: "At times, I have the impression that most politicians still do not understand that they are already under the control of financial markets, and are even dominated by them." Need I say more? Today, even Alan Greenspan, chairman of the Federal Reserve for so many years, expressed the same idea in his book *The Map and the Territory*.[2] Well, the social doctrine of the church cannot accept such a "division of roles." Politics must return to be the realm of ends, and between these three spheres there must be a systematic, and not improvised, cooperative relationship. There must be autonomy, of course, but not separation between them. And we must bear in mind that Catholic ethics is based on the Aristotelian-Thomist principle of the primacy of good over justice. Justice makes sense if it aims at accomplishing what is good; otherwise, it becomes judicialism. Postmodernity does not accept, as we know well, this vision. In its view, the rule, the norm, originates only from the consent of the parties involved, which should not refer to some "good" conception of life. Economic action is therefore based on the principle that *consensus facit iustum* (the mutual consent makes what is just), just as the system of libertarian individualism, predominant today, requires.

Are the paragraphs of Populorum Progressio, *stating that private property is not an absolute right but is subject to the common good, and the claims of the* Catechism of Saint Pius X, *according to which*

the sins that cry to heaven for vengeance are the oppression of the
poor and defrauding workers of their just wages, still valid today?

That private property cannot be considered an absolute right is
so obvious that even the great John Locke recognized this fact in
the second half of the seventeenth century. Rather, what needs
to be clarified is the distinction between "common good" and
"total good"—terms that are too often taken as equivalent. If the
"common good" is a product, in which the mulipliers are the good
of the individuals, the "total good" is more like a sum, in which
the addends represent the good of the individual persons. The
sense of this metaphor then is clear: according to the logic of the
"common good," we cannot sacrifice the welfare of someone to
better, no matter of how much, that of others; the product would
be zero. In a sum this is not the case. Further, the "common good"
is the good of all people—even of those who underperform—and
of the whole person in its three dimensions: the material, the
socio-relational, and the spiritual. The concept of "total good" is
a typical expression of utilitarianism; the "common good" instead
of one of the four pillars of the social doctrine of the church.

In today's globalized society, what are the possible applications and
implications of teachings that are not only social but are at the very
heart of the Christian faith?

In the current historical climate, the practical implications of the
teaching of the social doctrine of the church involve the recovery
of important pieces of that tradition of thought, asserted during the eighteenth century in Naples and Milan, which is civil
economy. On the one hand, we need to redesign the rules of the
game—that is, the institutions, especially the economic ones,
which are still largely of the "mining" type (to use the felicitous
expression coined by Daron Acemoğlu and James Robinson)—
that exclude citizens, instead of including them. On the other
hand, we must insert the principle of gift as gratuitousness—and
not as donation—within the economic discourse and practice,
giving life to all those economic initiatives that have *reciprocity* as

their regulative principle. I'm thinking here of social enterprises, productive associations, ethical finance, "voting with the wallet," institutional structures of corporate governance that include positive rights of participation of workers, and so on. It is a great encouragement to note that the model of civil economy is gaining momentum, perhaps more abroad than in Italy, where it actually originated. But already at the beginning of the nineteenth century our great poet Giacomo Leopardi, with his famous essay on the customs of the Italians, had already prepared us to this "peculiarity" of ours.

chapter 14

A VOICE FROM THE *VILLAS MISERIAS*

There is a criterion for knowing whether God is close to us or far away: all those who worry about the hungry, the naked, the poor, the disappeared, the tortured, the imprisoned—about any suffering human being—are close to God.

—Oscar Arnulfo Romero, Archbishop of San Salvador

Carlos Olivero, better known as Fr. Charly, is a priest who still goes around the neighborhoods of Buenos Aires in a black military jeep. On seeing him, his former archbishop, Jorge Mario Bergoglio, would have asked, still smiling, if he had escaped from the Vietnam War. Father Charly has worked with the poor and the marginalized of the Argentine capital since he was a seminarian. He is not a man of many words, and even more so of many theories or arguments. His experience as a "priest of the *villas miserias*" may help to understand Francis's own concern for the poor.

Father Charly came to Italy in the summer of 2014. It was his first time, and the occasion was the presentation of the book by Silvina Premat, *Preti dalla fine del mondo* (Priests From the End of the World).[1] The book tells the stories of priests involved in the *villas miserias*, "a very important reality," as Don Luigi Ciotti writes in the Italian preface, "if you want to understand the 'background' of Pope Francis."

The *villas miserias* are a phenomenon that first appeared a century ago. The expression refers to the urban slums woven into the urban fabric of Buenos Aires and other major Argentine cities, often built on illegal dumps or alongside contaminated water streams. Today they are mainly inhabited by immigrants from Paraguay and Bolivia, as well as by Argentine migrants from rural areas.

The traditon of the priests who take care of these people began in the years of the Second Vatican Council. But there is a twist to their story. The *curas villeros* (slum priests) had made their choice of life with the intention to change the situation in these slums. But they ended up being changed themselves, as they discovered the rich popular piety and deep faith of the people there who did not ask for trade unionists or political agitators; they just wanted priests in the true sense of the word.

"Sometimes," wrote Fr. Jorge Vernazza, a "pioneer" of the *curas villeros* who died in 1997, "among us we used to talk of seeking an 'authentic faith' . . . but it was the reality of the people of the *villas* with whom we dealt, generously and without prejudice, who eventually opened our eyes to the richness of the people's devotion."

So the priests started to build chapels—Santa María Madre del Pueblo in Bajo Flores, Cristo Obrero in Villa de Retiro, and Cristo Libertador in Villa 30—where they celebrated baptisms, marriages, and funerals, recited the rosary, and organized processions. At the same time they continued to work to improve the living conditions of their people, having to face in more recent years a terrible new monster, *el paco*, a cheap drug obtained from the chemical processing of cocaine that has devastating effects on the brain and ruins the lives of children and young people.

Father Charly, who before becoming a priest wanted to pursue a medical career, works primarily with the victims of *el paco*. And so the *Hogar de Cristo*, the rehabilitation centers for drug addicts in the villas, were opened. At the inauguration of the first of these centers in 2008, the then-Cardinal Bergoglio came to celebrate Mass on Holy Thursday, washing the feet of twelve of them. "He told us," recalled Fr. Charly, "that life must be welcomed as it is. Those few words have marked my path. It means that to welcome people we do not need moral, social, or any other kind of filter."

The most popular priest among the slums is Fr. Pepe di Paola, who for some years has been forced to leave the slums after receiving threats to his life by the narcos. He said: "In our neigh-borhoods they call us fathers and we are very proud of this title. We are fathers of a family and this family is our neighborhood. And as fathers we care and do what we can so that our families, our neighborhoods, prosper. A child or teen can call us father not only because he sees us wearing the clerical collar but because we care about him, so that he grows in a healthy way."

"In the 1960s and '70s—as reported in the book by Silvina Premat— the *curas villeros*, such as Fr. Daniel de la Sierra and the martyred priest Carlos Mugica, had to raise their powerless arms to block the bulldozers sent several times by military regimes to flatten the people's shacks. Even today among the priests of the *villas miserias*, the attempt to try to protect those beloved poor is almost a conditioned reflex or instinctive gesture. And in re-cent years, the most infamous dangers infiltrating the villas are the lower-cost drugs that take away the sparkle from the eyes, destroying the brains of young people, teenagers, children."

What are the traits of these priests? First of all, many of them expressly ask to go to serve in the villas, which in today's Buenos Aires amount to dangerous and crime-infested slums. And yet they are also places of extraordinary humanity encountered in the poorest conditions, with immigrants from neighboring countries (Paraguay, Bolivia, Peru) living together. Further, "they are priests who are faithfully following the examples of their predecessors. What a faithful of the parish of the villa 1/11/14 said of one of the first slum priests, Rodolfo Ricciardelli, applies to the others as well: 'He became a friend of the poor; he did not come to help the poor: those are two different things.' The slum priests are in close contact with the hardships and more immediate emergen-cies of their impoverished faithful: unemployment, drug addic-tion, violence, and drug dealing."

We met Fr. Charly in Milan, in a rare moment of pause on his long and strenuous Italian tour, on the eve of his return to Buenos Aires. We asked him what he thinks of the allegations of Marxism addressed to Pope Francis.

"I think that those who launched these accusations are ig-norant, in the sense that they ignore reality. . . . The world revolving around money does not know what to do with Jesus' message. But it is inconceivable that private property is a value considered more important than the life of a man or a woman; it just cannot be. I share the pope's concerns, and I recognize that this is barbaric."

We then asked him whether he is surprised to hear the harsh criticisms directed toward Francis's words on poverty and on the "economy that kills." Father Charly shakes his head.

> No, I'm not surprised at all. It is only logical that those who hold in their hands the destiny of the world do not want a system different from the one that is most convenient for their own interests. Their reaction seems logical; it is the logic of their thinking. They are trying to discredit the possibility of another social system. The pope says very clearly that this system can no longer work and that we must build a new civilization. So they try to discredit him, and if they do not do it with ignorance, they do it with evil intent in order to create confusion. I repeat, I am not surprised that the centers of power accuse him in this way.

But there are not only the allegations of Marxism coming from some quarters, especially American ones. There is even a certain intra-ecclesial distancing from what is branded as "pauperism": in short, for some within the church itself, Francis speaks too much of the poor.

> This accusation of pauperism and the resistance to the pope's message has to do with the history of the last decades. And yet, the option for the poor, the work with the poor, the understanding that the church must focus on the poorest are tenets that have been part of the life of the church in all ages. If one reads St. John Chrysostom, you will find passages that are remarkable in this regard. If one considers, for example, the collection that St. Paul took up, or the first chapters of the Acts of the Apostles, it seems to me that these accusations, these resistances, even within the church, are unjustified. They are the result of a mentality that has its roots in the history of the last thirty to forty years. But the concern for the poor has always been part of the life of the church and of the gospel message. There has always

been the belief that identifies the poor as those deserving more attention. The pope is in this line, and it seems to me that in this way he is proposing a return to the spirit of the gospel.

We then ask Fr. Charly, who as a priest has always served in the *villas miserias,* celebrating Mass and helping drug addicts in the streets, whether he has ever been accused of being "ideological" or "political"?

> No, nobody has ever raised such a direct and serious accusation against me. Maybe at times it came out as prejudice. . . . I work with kids with drug problems. The drug that circulates in the *villas miserias* of Buenos Aires is called *el paco*; these kids are living a situation of extreme social exclusion and in order to be saved, to give them a chance to change, it is not enough to offer them a path of recovery. We must also change the world around them, creating opportunities for them, dealing with hospitals that do not want to accept them, dealing with the authorities that do not want to issue documents for them, and trying to find for them some money, a job, and a house. There must be a community that supports and accompanies them.

"Our work," continued Fr. Charly, telling us about the commitment of the community of priests to which he belongs,

> is not only dedicated to the person who we help; sometimes it is also directed to the various state offices and structures, to generate accessibility. . . . In Buenos Aires we speak very often of evangelization of the state. We talked about this with Bergoglio, when he was still our archbishop: to "evangelize" the state means to help the state occupy the place it should have, and do its job. Is this a political activity? Yes, perhaps, but certainly it is nonpartisan and nonsectarian. The concept is very close to the principle of subsidiarity, which seeks to give back to the state the place it should have in order to be a part of the life of its citizens. It must subsidize . . . make a contribution to improve citizens' lives. We also work to help the state find its role. Because otherwise our kids would continue to be excluded from it all!

"Here's an example," added Fr. Charly.

> We work with girls who take drugs, and to be able to buy drugs they prostitute themselves. By doing so, they get sick, are exposed to the HIV virus and hepatitis, and become pregnant. It is very important that hospital maternity wards accept them, because if they don't the child is bought by drug traffickers. We work with hospital maternity wards, and together we made a journey. At first these girls were rejected, but now they're accepted. And we accompany them; we help them so that they can keep their child. We seek for them a place where they can live and learn to become mothers. Can our commitment be considered "political"? I don't know; it concerns the life of the common people. But for sure we don't do partisan politics.

What is most striking in meeting these priests who work in the *villas miserias* is the lack of any ideological stance. Their dedication to the poor is simply the consequence of the faith they live, and from their stories emerge their surprise and their gratitude for the testimony of faith they receive from the Christian people for whom they care.

"In the villas," explained Fr. Charly,

> it is truly awesome. It is a faith that is expressed in pilgrimages, in the devotion to the saints, and in so many other different and rich ways; it is a faith that teaches hospitality. I remember that, when I was studying the history of the church, I was struck by these words in the Rule of St. Benedict: "All guests who arrive be received as Christ, because He will say: 'I was a stranger and you welcomed me.' And let due honor be shown to all." The people of the villas have this sense of hospitality that is profoundly Christian. Otherwise one cannot explain why in the city people live shut in their homes, in fear and insecurity, while here it's so different. People in the villas live with the doors open. They welcome their neighbors over for dinner, so they can sit down and eat something. They share half a pack of rice with that neighbor whose husband is unemployed. And Sunday is the day of rest. The men gather to help neighbors fix their houses because they have no money to pay construction workers. . . . These are just a few examples of everyday life.

"Solidarity, hospitality," continued the Argentine priest,

> are Christian "seeds"—seeds of that same Christianity that is
> expressed in the devotion to the saints and the veneration of the
> Virgin Mary. At the rescue center we try to involve everyone in a
> communal atmosphere: the same kids who are on a journey of
> recovery are invited by others: we ask those who have been in
> recovery for two months to go visit those who are in jail deprived
> of their freedom. To those who lived on the streets and now have
> a place to stay, we ask that they welcome someone else still on
> the streets to sleep over. . . . To others who have a little time
> to spare we ask them to go to the hospital to help a patient who
> has difficulty eating alone. To watch out for one another for us
> means to build a community—a community whose foundation is
> the gospel. It is the evangelical life that supports the community.

"The complete opposite of this way of life," explained Fr.
Charly is the

> individualism that is locking people in their own homes. That
> individualism that leads people to think that they should get all
> the convenience and comfort for themselves, their children, their
> wives and husbands. . . . A narrow-mindedness that makes you
> think that your neighbor is not your brother or sister. Christianity
> means communal life, and if someone thinks of communal life
> as an evangelical life, that person is welcoming. If one thinks
> instead that the first experience of Christianity is moral or doc-
> trinal, this one excludes and separates, because you are going
> to look at what others practice or don't practice, what they do
> or don't do, what they believe or don't believe. Instead, starting
> from community life as evangelical experience is very good for
> people. Everyone feels accepted and part of a real family.

The starting point is always the reality one lives. And in the
case of the *villas miserias*, it is the faith, the popular devotion.
"People's faith," said the Argentine priest, "tells you a lot. What
we realize every day is that the people of our neighborhoods
have a vision of faith capable of embracing all aspects of life. A
disease is interpreted spiritually. The illness of a family member

turns into a call to God and becomes a prayer. The lack of work, when people go to seek help from San Cayetano, becomes a turning to God. . . . All life is a turning to God. The faithful don't relegate themselves to worship alone; their faith does not end with worship."

Father Charly rejects the idea that the believer should be silent in the face of what is happening.

> This idea that our Catholic faith prevents us from intervening in the injustices of the world, of that same world that we have built, represents a view that is "cultic," narrow, limited, and dissociated from life. An idea that is the fruit of the individualistic culture that insists on relegating faith to the private and personal sphere. Faith, however, has to do with all aspects of life. All life is related to God. There are many of our brothers and sisters who have nothing to eat. This is also true for Europe, as I've been able to see. The message is extremely clear: we have built such an unequal world that now there seems to be a movement back to the well-off countries. As I've been walking around the streets of Italy, I've seen a huge number of immigrants; these are people who have come to find something to eat. Evidently, the current capitalist system, as it is, is no good.

"How can we allow this to continue? How can we not think about ways to change all this?" asked Fr. Charly. His words are reminiscent of the relevance and strength of certain Catholic social teachings—teachings that the same Catholics often forget. "When the magisterium of the church speaks of the expropriation of large unused estates, for us in South America that is a very strong message! Not even today's Marxists talk about confiscating large unused estates: it is inconceivable that in this day and age property is considered more important than life itself. It is normal then that those who defend this system only want it to last and are troubled when they hear certain statements. We should not be surprised by those allegations against Pope Francis."

chapter 15

IN FRANCIS'S OWN WORDS

Is it pauperism? No, it is the gospel!

> *Do you want to honor Christ's body? Then do not scorn him in his nakedness, nor honor him here in the church with silken garments while neglecting him outside where he is cold and naked.*
>
> —St. John Chrysostom

Marxist. Communist. Pauperist. Francis's words on poverty and social justice, together with his frequent calls for concern for the needy, have drawn criticism and even accusations sometimes expressed, as we have seen, with harshness and sarcasm. How does Pope Francis feel about this? Why is the issue of poverty so central to his teachings? At the end of this journey through Pope Francis's interventions in the first two years of his pontificate, we have asked some questions directly to him. What follows are his answers.

Your Holiness, is the most recent form of capitalism, the one we are living today, a somewhat irreversible system?

I would not know how to answer this question. I recognize that globalization has helped to lift many people out of poverty, but it has also condemned many others to die of hunger. True, in absolute terms global wealth has increased, but so have inequalities and new forms of poverty. What I have noticed is that this system sustains itself through a culture of waste, of which I have already spoken several times. Today, we are witnessing the emergence of a politics, a sociology, and even an attitude of waste. When at the core of the system humanity is replaced by money, and when money becomes an idol, men and women are reduced to mere instruments of a social and economic system character-ized—better yet *dominated*—by profound imbalances. Thus, we discard whatever does not serve this logic; it is the same attitude that allows us to discard children and the elderly, and this atti-tude now affects the young as well. I was shocked to learn that there are many millions of young people under twenty-five in developed countries who are jobless. I call them the "neither-nor" generation, because they neither study nor work. They do not study because they are not given the opportunity to do so; they do not work because there are no jobs. But I would also like to draw attention to that aspect of the culture of waste that leads people to dispose of babies through abortion. I am astonished by the low birth rates here in Italy; this is how we lose our link to the future. Similarly, the culture of waste leads to a "hidden euthanasia" of the elderly, who are abandoned instead of being considered our memory, a link to our own past and a source of wisdom for our present. I often wonder what will be discarded next. We need to stop before it is too late. Let us stop this, please! Therefore, getting back to your question, I would say that we should not consider this state of things irreversible. Let us not resign to it. Let us try to build a society and an economy where people and their well-being, not money, are at the core.

Can a more ethical economic system—led by men and women who care about the common good—bring about change and a greater focus on social justice and the redistribution of wealth? Or is it also right to hypothesize a restructuring of the system?

First of all, we need to remember that there is need for more eth-ics in the economy, and there is need for more ethics in politics. Various heads of state and political leaders, whom I have met after my election as Bishop of Rome, have often talked to me about this. They told me that we, as religious leaders, should help them by giving them ethical instruction. True, pastors can make their pleas, but I am convinced that we need, as Benedict XVI recalled in the encyclical *Caritas in Veritate*, men and women with their arms raised in prayer toward God, knowing that love and sharing, which creates genuine development, are not the fruit of our hands, but a gift to ask for. And, at the same time, I am convinced that there is a need for these men and women to commit themselves on every level—in society, in politics, in institutions, and in the economy—working for the common good. We can no longer wait to fix the structural causes of poverty, to cure our society from a disease that can only lead to new crises. Markets and financial speculation cannot enjoy absolute autonomy. Without a solution to the problems of the poor, we will not be able to find a solution for the world's problems. We need programs, structures, and policies leading to a better allocation of resources, job creation, and the integral advancement of those who are excluded.

How important is it for Christians to recover a sense of care for creation and sustainable development? And how may we ensure that this is not confused with a certain environmentalist ideology that considers humanity the real threat for the well-being of our planet?

Even for the protection of creation we must overcome the culture of waste. Creation is the gift that God has given to humanity so it can be protected, cultivated, used for our livelihood, and handed over to future generations. The vocation to take care of someone or something is human, before being Christian, and affects all; we are called to care for creation, its beauty, and to respect all creatures of God and the environment in which we live. If we fail in this responsibility, if we do not take care of our brothers and sisters and of all creation, destruction will advance. Unfortunately, we must remember that every period of history has its own "Herods" who destroy, plot schemes of death, and disfigure the face of man and woman, destroying creation. Humanity has received as gift—as Romano Guardini pointed out—this "ignorance" and turned it into culture. But when humanity, instead of being custodian, considers itself to be the master, it becomes creator of a second "ignorance" and moves toward destruction. Consider nuclear weapons and the possibility to annihilate in a few instants a huge number of people. Consider also genetic manipulation, the manipulation of life, or gender theory that does not recognize the order of creation. Think about those who restore the tower of Babel and destroy creation. This attitude leads humanity to commit a new sin against God the Creator. The real protection of creation has nothing to do with ideologies that consider humanity an accident or a problem to be eliminated. God has placed men and women at the head of creation and has entrusted them with the earth. The design of God the Creator is inscribed in nature.

In your opinion, why do Pius XI's strong and prophetic words, in his encyclical Quadragesimo Anno, *against the international imperialism of money sound to many—even Catholics—exaggerated and radical today?*

Pius XI seems exaggerated only to those who feel struck by his words and hit where it hurts by his prophetic condemnations. But Pius XI was not exaggerating; he only told the truth after the economic and financial crisis of 1929, and, as a good mountaineer, he saw things as they were; he could look ahead. I am afraid that the only ones who are exaggerating are the ones who still feel called into question by Pius XI's reproaches.

Are the paragraphs of Populorum Progressio, *stating that private property is not an absolute right but is subject to the common good, and the claims of the* Catechism of Saint Pius X, *according to which the sins that cry to heaven for vengeance are the oppression of the poor and defrauding workers of their just wages, still valid today?*

Not only are they still valid, but the more time goes on, the more I find that they have been proven by experience.

Because of some passages of the exhortation Evangelii Gaudium, *a critic from the United States has accused you of being a Marxist. How does it feel to be considered a follower of Karl Marx?*

As I have mentioned earlier, I have met many Marxists in my life who are good people, so I don't feel offended by these comments. But Marxist ideology is wrong.

The sentence of Evangelii Gaudium *that most struck a chord was the one about an economy that "kills."*

And yet, in the exhortation I did not say anything that is not already in the teachings of the social doctrine of the church. Also, I didn't speak from a technical point of view. I simply tried to present a picture of what happens. The only specific reference was to the so-called "trickle-down" economic theories, according to which every economic growth, encouraged by a free market, will inevitably bring about greater equity and global inclusiveness. The promise was that when the glass was full, it would have flowed over and the poor would have benefited from it. Instead, what happens is that when the glass is full it mysteriously gets larger, and so nothing ever comes out of it for the poor. This was the only reference to a specific theory. I repeat, I do not speak as an economical expert, but according to the social doctrine of the church. And this does not mean that I am a Marxist. Perhaps whoever has made this comment does not know the social doctrine of the church and, apparently, does not even know Marxism all that well either.

Your words about the poor as the "flesh of Christ" and your emphasis on the fact that the care for the poor is at the heart of the Christian message, and not just a sociological fact, have touched a chord with many people. You have also spoken about this at Assisi, inviting all to worship the body of Christ in the Eucharist and to touch the flesh of Christ in disabled people. Are you bothered by the charges of "pauperism"?

Before Francis of Assisi, in the Middle Ages there were the "paupers," as well as many pauperistic currents. Pauperism is a caricature of the gospel and of poverty itself. Instead, St. Francis helped us to discover the profound link between poverty and the ways of the gospel. Jesus says that we cannot serve two masters, God and wealth. Is this pauperism? Jesus tells us what the "protocol" is on which we will be judged, as written in chapter 25 of Matthew's gospel: I was hungry, I was thirsty, I was in prison, I was sick, I was naked and you helped me, clothed me, visited me, and took care of me. Every time we do this to our brother or sister, we do it to Jesus. Caring for our neighbor, the poor, those who suffer in body and spirit, those in need: this is the touchstone. Is it pauperism? No, it's the gospel. Poverty protects us from idolatry, from self-sufficiency. Zacchaeus, after meeting Jesus' merciful gaze, donated half of his possessions to the poor. The gospel message is for all; the gospel does not condemn the rich but the idolatry of wealth, that idolatry that makes us insensitive to the cry of the poor. Jesus said that before offering our gift at the altar we must reconcile ourselves with our brother and sister to be at peace with him. I believe that, by analogy, we can also extend this request to being at peace with our poor brothers and sisters.

You have stressed the continuity with the tradition of the church in its concern for the poor. To conclude, can you give us some more examples?

A month before the opening of the Second Vatican Council, Pope John XXIII said: "The church reveals itself as it is and as it aspires to be, that is, everyone's church, and particularly the church of the poor." In the following years, the preferential option for the poor has emerged in the documents of the magisterium. Some might think of it as something new, but it is a concern that originates in the gospel and is documented in the early centuries of Christianity. If I repeated some passages from the homilies of the early fathers of the church—say, of the second or third century—about how we should treat the poor, there would certainly be someone saying that my homily is Marxist. "You are not making a gift of what is yours to the poor, but you are giving back what is theirs. You have been appropriating things that are meant to be for the common use of everyone. The earth belongs to everyone, not to the rich." These are St. Ambrose's words, which Pope Paul VI cited in *Populorum Progressio* to affirm that private property does not constitute an absolute and unconditioned right for anyone and that, when others lack basic necessities, no one is justified in keeping for one's exclusive use what is not needed. Saint John Chrysostom wrote: "Not sharing your goods with the poor means robbing them and depriving them of their life. What we possess is not ours, but theirs." And further: Do you want to honor Christ's body? Then do not scorn him in his nakedness, nor honor him here in the church with silken garments while neglecting him outside where he is cold and naked (Homily 50 on Matthew). He who said: This is my Body, also said: I was hungry and and you gave me no food." As you can see, this concern for the poor is in the gospel, and it is within the tradition of the church. It is not an invention of communism, and we must not turn it into an ideology, as sometimes has happened in the course of history. The church's invitation to overcome what I have called the "globalization of indifference" is far from any political interest and ideology. Animated only by Jesus' words, the church wants to make its contribution to build a world where we look after one another and care for each other.

Epilogue

THE ECONOMY AND THE GOSPEL

Reclaiming the past to build the future

*The need to resolve the structural causes of poverty cannot
be delayed, not only for the pragmatic reason of its urgency
for the good order of society, but because society needs to be
cured of a sickness which is weakening and frustrating it,
and which can only lead to new crises.*

—Pope Francis, *Evangelii Gaudium*

"Markets and financial speculation cannot enjoy absolute autonomy," says Pope Francis in the interview published in the preceding pages. "Without a solution to the problems of the poor, we will not be able to find a solution for the world's problems." In continuity with the tradition of the social doctrine of the church, and without neglecting some of its most significant and prophetic pages, Francis tells us that if we do not solve the problems of the poor by, on the one hand, giving up the absolute autonomy of markets and financial speculation and, on the other, attacking the structural causes of inequality, "no solution will be found for the world's problems or, for that matter, to any problems." Because "inequality is the root of social ills."

The critical tone of the pope's exhortation *Evangelii Gaudium* and that of other documents of his magisterium has had great media coverage and sparked, as we have seen, many reactions.

It is worth mentioning again, at the end of our journey, that at the heart of Francis's programmatic document there is the "pastoral conversion" of a church struggling for renewal and openness to the outer world in order to proclaim to all the joy of the gospel. *Evangelii Gaudium* is most of all an exhortation that does not have the intention to systematize a thought, let alone an economic one, but it realistically points to some of the evils that are there for everyone to see, as it wants to promote a transformation of the church and of Christians. Therefore, we cannot separate the social and economic passages of *Evangelii Gaudium* from its overall message. Examining the homilies of the church fathers with a clear social message, Wendy Mayer notes that beyond the primary recipients there is always an evangelizing purpose in those homilies. "According to the church fathers," writes Jesuit Fr. Diego Alonso-Lasheras, "a serious engagement of Christians in the social world would not only be advantageous, as it would allow them to live their faith more deeply, but it would also have a missiological and evangelizing effect on non-Christians. With *Evangelii Gaudium*, Francis is going in the same direction, and to that effect he wants the whole church to experience the joy of evangelizing—in the social sphere and, consequently, in economic relations as well."[1]

As it often happens, even in the case of this papal document, most of the attention went to the more openly critical passages—if only because none of today's world leaders seem really interested in putting their finger on the problem of poverty and inequality and inquiring into its causes and possible solutions—at the expense of the more proactive ones(e.g., those paragraphs that directly call Christians to strive to improve the land they inhabit as part of humanity's common home). It is for this reason that Francis recalled the statement made by Paul VI's apostolic letter *Octogesima Adveniens*, when he says that it is up to Christian communities to speak in their own particular voices as they face different situations, analyzing objectively the social circumstances in which they live in order to look at them in the light of the gospel. It is a much-needed reminder. On many of the most recent issues in the contemporary debate—for example, the problem of speculative finance in relation to the current cri-sis—we hardly ever hear of reflections and proposals coming from Christian communities. Perhaps this is due, as is the case in Italy, to the increasingly marginal role played by the episcopal heirarchy in the last decades.

"The dignity of each human person and the pursuit of the com-mon good," as stated in *Evangelii Gaudium*, "are concerns which ought to shape all economic policies. At times, however, they seem to be a mere addendum imported from without in order to fill out a political discourse lacking in perspectives or plans for true and integral development." Growth in justice "requires more than economic growth, while presupposing such growth: it requires decisions, programmes, mechanisms and processes specifically geared to a better distribution of income, the creation of sources of employment and an integral promotion of the poor which goes beyond a simple welfare mentality." In short, it requires men and women who look to the future, who are committed to pursue the common good and whose goal is not just the next election campaign. It requires men and women who not only look at the spread and stock market indices as indicators of the health of a country but inquire whether the younger generations have a job, a future, and hope; whether children have kindergartens and schools that can educate them by introducing them to reality; whether couples have the opportunity to buy a house; whether there are effective welfare programs available for the elderly; and whether those who still bet on the future by putting children into the world are justly taxed, rather than penalized. It requires men and women who are engaged in politics and work in institutions without corrupting themselves or letting others corrupt them, even managing perhaps to revive a minimum of esteem (which has never been so in decline) for that "highest form of charity"—that is, politics—inasmuch as it is exclusively committed to the com-mon good and to the real lives of people, with special attention and dedication to those in difficulty, those left behind, those who are excluded and should instead be included.

We will now recall those principles, already mentioned and discussed at the end of chapter 4, and that Pope Francis has repeatedly mentioned and discussed. First, *time is greater than space*. This means that we need to work on the long term, focusing on processes rather than occupying spaces of power, giving priority to new social initiatives involving other people and other groups that will make them their own and carry them forward. Second, *unity prevails over conflict*. This means that conflicts inevitably emerge, and when they do, they should be managed by resolving them in a new synthesis of diversity. Third, *realities are more important than ideas*. This is a principle as timely as ever in a world that still pays the price of various ideologies that have imposed their categories on reality instead of starting from it. Imposing abstract ideas, models, and strategies can corrupt politics as well as the economy, ending in irrationality, lack of common sense, and being out of touch with the experience of ordinary people. Fourth, and last, *the whole is greater than the part*. "With this principle," explained Fr. Alonso-Lasheras, "the pope wants to prevent us from falling into two possible extremes: on the one hand, an abstract and globalized universalism; on the other, a folkloristic localism incapable of being challenged by what is new and different."[2]

Francis has proposed these principles in an evangelical key, but they can also apply to the economy and the economic sciences. "The economy and the economic sciences," continues Fr. Alonso-Lasheras in his reflections on *Evangelii Gaudium*,

> are invited to not lose sight of their ability to initiate processes that can include more and more people in the economy; an economy that must increasingly and more efficiently provide the necessary means for a decent life to as many people as possible. The economy and the economic sciences are invited to see the profound unity of economic processes that must prevail over conflict and competition. The market is not only the place where producers, sellers, and consumers enter into competition. The market is also an expression of a community that enables and supports the economic performance; the community is a moral-ecological niche that sustains the life of a legal and economic institution like that of the market. The economy and the economic sciences are invited to build a discourse in which

economic ideas are always in dialogue with reality, instead of concealing it; economic ideas that engage, and not just classify and define; economic ideas that take into account the life and the economic rationality of real people. Finally, the economy and the economic sciences are invited to hold together globalization and localization, sinking the roots of economic activity in the fertile soil of its own history and its own native place, both intended as gifts of God but with an open outlook toward a global economy.

This final invitation questions primarily those dealing specifically with the economy, those who work in the markets, and those who manage them. But it also addresses politicians, who cannot inertly continue to twiddle their thumbs, remaining submissive to economic and financial mechanisms and continuing to be ruled by the markets rather than govern for the good of the citizens and the real people. And, finally, it is a call to all Christians and to all those of goodwill, so they may come out of their "bubbles" of indifference, get involved in the life of their communities, and find the courage to ask their political leaders for commitment and wide-ranging projects in an attempt to build, for those who live today and for future generations, a more just and inclusive society.

NOTES

Preface: Is the Pope a Marxist? (pages vii–xiii)

1. Pope Francis, *Evangelii Gaudium,* encyclical on the proclamation of the gospel, November 24, 2013, no. 53–54, http://w2.vatican.va /content/francesco/en/apost_exhortations/documents/papa-francesco _esortazione-ap_20131124_evangelii-gaudium.html.

2. Translator's Note: The word "pauperist" is used in a denigratory manner to refer to someone who supports and embraces—often exaggeratedly or conceitedly—material poverty.

3. Translator's Note: After Francis's election to the papacy, the word "pauperism" has been used in the sense of policies and principles promoting material poverty as opposed to a broader and more evangelical notion of poverty intended as freedom and detachment from goods and possessions.

Chapter 1: A Poor Church for the Poor (pages 1–7)

1. Pope Francis, Audience to Representatives of the Communications Media, March 16, 2013, https://w2.vatican.va/content/francesco/en /speeches/2013/march/documents/papa-francesco_20130316_rappre sentanti-media.html.

2. Pope Francis, Address on the Vigil of Pentecost with the Ecclesial Movements, May 18, 2013, http://w2.vatican.va/content/francesco /en/speeches/2013/may/documents/papa-francesco_20130518_veglia -pentecoste.html.

Chapter 2: The Imperialism of Money (pages 8–18)

1. Gianni Valente, "Il volto idolatra dell'economia speculativa," *30 Days,* no. 1 (January 2002): 19–21.

2. ZENIT, "Cardinal Bergoglio's Lenten Message for Buenos Aires," March 14, 2013, http://www.zenit.org/en/articles/cardinal-bergoglio

-s-lenten-message-for-buenos-aires/. The English translation, however, omits the portion related to "violence that kills and destroys families."

Chapter 3: The Globalization of Indifference (pages 19–30)

1. Pope Francis, homily, Salina Quarter, Lampedusa, July 8, 2013, http://w2.vatican.va/content/francesco/en/homilies/2013/documents/papa-francesco_20130708_omelia-lampedusa.html.

2. Francis, Address to Workers, Largo Carlo Felice, Cagliari, Sardinia, September 22, 2013, http://w2.vatican.va/content/francesco/en/speeches/2013/september/documents/papa-francesco_20130922_lavoratori-cagliari.html.

3. Francis, Address to the Centesimus Annus Pro Pontifice Foundation, May 25, 2013, http://w2.vatican.va/content/francesco/en/speeches/2013/may/documents/papa-francesco_20130525_centesimus-annus-pro-pontifice.html.

4. Francis, Address to the Community of Varginha, Manguinhos, Rio de Janiero, July 25, 2013, http://w2.vatican.va/content/francesco/en/speeches/2013/july/documents/papa-francesco_20130725_gmg-comunita-varginha.html.

5. Francis, "No to 'slave labour'," morning meditation in the chapel of the *Domus Sanctae Marthae*, May 1, 2013, http://w2.vatican.va/content/francesco/en/cotidie/2013/documents/papa-francesco-cotidie_20130501_slave-labour.html.

6. Francis, Address to the Managers and Workers of the Terni Steel Mill and the Faithful of the Diocese of Terni-Narni-Amelia, Italy, March 20, 2014, http://w2.vatican.va/content/francesco/en/speeches/2014/march/documents/papa-francesco_20140320_pellegrinaggio-diocesi-terni.html.

Chapter 4: Such an Economy Kills (pages 31–46)

1. Pope Francis, *Evangelii Gaudium,* encyclical on the proclamation of the gospel, November 24, 2013, http://w2.vatican.va/content/francesco/en/apost_exhortations/documents/papa-francesco_esortazione-ap_20131124_evangelii-gaudium.html.

2. Gian Paolo Salvini, "Uno Sguardo sulla Società con la 'Evangelii Gaudium'," *La Civiltà Cattolica* 39/29 (2014): 509.

3. Ibid., 509.

4. Ibid., 510.

5. Diego Alonso-Lasheras, "Evangelizzazione ed economia: denuncia e proposta," in *Evangelii gaudium: il testo ci interroga,* ed. Humberto Miguel Yañez (Rome: Gregorian & Biblical Press, 2014), 227.

6. Salvini, "Uno Sguardo sulla Società," 512.

7. Ibid., 514.

8. Ibid., 515.

9. Ibid., 515–16.

Chapter 5: Allegations against a "Marxist Pope"
(pages 47–68)

1. Diego Alonso-Lasheras, "Evangelizzazione ed economia: denuncia e proposta," in *Evangelii gaudium: il testo ci interroga,* ed. Humberto Miguel Yañez (Rome: Gregorian & Biblical Press, 2014), 226.

2. Interview with Cardinal Raymond L. Burke, *The World Over with Raymond Arroyo,* EWTN, December 12, 2013, https://www.youtube.com /watch?v=Edq69fJLnXo/.

3. "It's Sad How Wrong Pope Francis Is (Unless It's a Deliberate Mistranslation by Leftists)," *The Rush Limbaugh Show,* November 27, 2013, http://www.rushlimbaugh.com/daily/2013/11/27/it_s_sad _how_wrong_pope_francis_is_unless_it_s_a_deliberate_mistranslation _by_leftists/.

4. Jonathan Moseley, "The Plain Truth: Jesus Christ Is a Capitalist," *WorldNetDaily*, December 1, 2013, http://www.wnd.com/2013/12 /jesus-christ-is-a-capitalist/.

5. Adam Shaw, "Pope Francis is the Catholic Church's Obama—God help us," Fox News: Opinion, December 4, 2013, http://www.foxnews .com/opinion/2013/12/04/pope-francis-is-catholic-churchs-obama-god -help-us.html; Katie Glueck, "The Francis Factor: Pope's economic ideas rattle GOP," *Politico,* December 25, 2013, http://www.politico.com /story/2013/12/pope-francis-catholic-church-republicans-gop-economics -101522.html; Bill Glauber, "Paul Ryan signals support for Kenosha casino," *Milwaukee Journal Sentinel,* December 19, 2013, http://www .jsonline.com/news/statepolitics/paul-ryan-signals-support-for-kenosha -casino-b99167734z1-236595381.html.

6. Michael Novak, *The Spirit of Democratic Capitalism* (New York: Simon & Schuster, 1982).

7. Michael Novak, "Agreeing with Pope Francis," *National Review*, December 7, 2013, http://www.nationalreview.com/article/365720 /agreeing-pope-francis-michael-novak/.

8. Massimo Borghesi, "Lo schiaffo di Francesco ai catto-capitalisti Usa," *Il Sussidiario*, January 3, 2014, http://www.ilsussidiario.net /News/Cultura/2014/1/3/PAPA-Borghesi-lo-schiaffo-di-Francesco-ai -catto-capitalisti-Usa/2/455907/.

9. Qtd. in James Pethokoukis, "A JP Morgan economist (in effect) responds to Pope Francis," blogpost @ *AEIdeas*, American Enterprise Institute, December 2, 2013, http://www.aei.org/publication/a-jp-morgan -economist-in-effect-responds-to-pope-francis/.

10. John Gapper, "Capitalism: In search of balance," *Financial Times*, December 23, 2013, http://www.ft.com/cms/s/0/4a0b8168-6bc0-11e3 -a216-00144feabdc0.html.

11. Alessandro Corneli, "Il Financial Times contro Papa Francesco," *Global Research & Reports Group,* December 26, 2013, http://grrg .eu/2013/12/il-financial-times-papa-francesco/.

12. Qtd. in Manzin Mauro, "Il cardinale sloveno Rode attacca Papa Bergoglio," *Il Piccolo*, September 28, 2014, http://ricerca.gelocal.it /ilpiccolo/archivio/ilpiccolo/2014/09/28/PR_10_08.html.

13. Qtd. in Laurie Goodstein, "Bishops Select Two Leaders Who Reflect New Tone Set by Pope," *New York Times*, November 12, 2013, http://www.nytimes.com/2013/11/13/us/kentucky-archbishop-joseph -e-kurtz-chosen-to-lead-us-bishops.html.

14. Qtd. in Catholic Diocese of Spokane, Washington, "Questions about involvement in the 40 Days for Life Program," news release, September 16, 2011, http://www.dioceseofspokane.org/bjc_2011 /bjc091611.htm.

15. "A bishop who can speak without shouting: Blase Cupich's reasonable voice on the mandate," *U.S. Catholic* (blog), Feb 17, 2012, http:// www.uscatholic.org/blog/2012/02/bishop-who-can-speak-without -shouting-blase-cupichs-reasonable-voice-mandate/.

16. Qtd. in Kevin J. Jones, "Next Chicago archbishop aims to nourish faith," Catholic News Agency, http://www.catholicnewsagency.com /news/next-chicago-archbishop-aims-to-nourish-faith-95074/.

17. Kishore Jayabalan, "Letter from Rome: Economic Liberty's Episcopal Discontents," Acton Institute for the Study of Religion and Liberty, October 1, 2014, http://www.acton.org/global/article/letter-rome -economic-liberty%E2%80%99s-episcopal-disconten/.

18. Mary Ann Walsh, "The Role of an Archbishop: An Interview with Cardinal Francis George," *America,* October 28, 2014, http://americamagazine .org/content/all-things/role-archbishop-interview-cardinal-francis-george/.

Chapter 6: A Finance That Feeds on Itself (pages 69–80)

1. Diego Alonso-Lasheras, "Evangelizzazione ed economia: denuncia e proposta," in *Evangelii gaudium: il testo ci interroga,* ed. Humberto Miguel Yáñez (Rome: Gregorian & Biblical Press, 2014), 229.

2. Gonzalo Fanjul, *Children of the Recession: The impact of the economic crisis on child well-being in rich countries,* Innocenti Report Card 12: Children in the Developed World, ed. Rick Boychuk (Florence: UNICEF Office of Research, 2014), http://www.unicef-irc.org/publications/pdf/rc12-eng-web.pdf.

3. Qtd. in UNICEF, "2.6 million more children plunged into poverty in rich countries during Great Recession," news release, October 28, 2014, http://www.unicef.org/media/media_76447.html.

4. Marion Fourcade, Philippe Steiner, Wolfgang Streeck, and Cornelia Woll, *Moral Categories in the Financial Crisis,* MaxPo Discussion Paper 13/1, Max Planck Sciences Po Center on Coping with Instability in Market Societies, June 2013, http://www.maxpo.eu/pub/maxpo_dp/maxpodp13-1.pdf.

5. Alonso-Lasheras, 229.

6. Pontifical Council for Justice and Peace, "Towards Reforming the International Financial and Monetary Systems in the Context of Global Public Authority," October 24, 2011, http://www.vatican.va/roman_curia/pontifical_councils/justpeace/documents/rc_pc_justpeace_doc_20111024_nota_en.html.

7. JP Morgan Chase, *The Euro area adjustment: about halfway there,* 2, 12, http://www.europe-solidarity.eu/documents/ES1_euro-area-adjustment.pdf.

8. Andrea Baranes, *Dobbiamo restituire fiducia ai mercati. Falso!* (Bari: Laterza, 2014).

9. Moryo Longo, "Le banche tornano a fabbricare titoli 'tosici'," *Il Sole 24 Ore,* June 6, 2013, http://www.ilsole24ore.com/art/finanza-e-mercati/2013-06-06/banche-tornano-fabbricare-titoli-064335.shtml.

10. Paul Krugman, "Unproductive Finance," *New York Times,* June 12, 2013, http://krugman.blogs.nytimes.com/2013/06/12/unproductive-finance/.

11. Joseph E. Stiglitz, *Freefall: America, Free Markets, and the Sinking of the World Economy* (New York: W. W. Norton, 2010), 2.

12. Robert B. Reich, *Aftershock: The Next Economy and America's Future* (New York: Vintage, 2011), 1.

13. Pontifical Council for Justice and Peace, "Towards Reforming."

14. Qtd. in Maria Claudia Ferragni, "Gregg: i poveri ci chiedono più mercato," *La Nuova Bussola Quotidiana,* August 14, 2014, http://www .lanuovabq.it/it/articoli-gregg-i-poverici-chiedonopiu-mercato-10023.htm

15. Pope Francis, Address to the New Non-Resident Ambassadors to the Holy See: Kyrgyzstan, Antigua and Barbuda, Luxembourg and Botswana, May 16, 2013, http://w2.vatican.va/content/francesco /en/speeches/2013/may/documents/papa-francesco_20130516_nuovi -ambasciatori.html.

16. Francis, Address to Participants in the 38th Conference of the Food and Agriculture Organization of the United Nations (FAO), June 20, 2013, http://w2.vatican.va/content/francesco/en/speeches/2013/june /documents/papa-francesco_20130620_38-sessione-fao.html.

17. Francis, Message for the Celebration of the World Day of Peace, January 1, 2014, http://w2.vatican.va/content/francesco/en/messages /peace/documents/papa-francesco_20131208_messaggio-xlvii-giornata -mondiale-pace-2014.html.

Chapter 7: American Theocon Criticism . . . of Benedict XVI? (pages 81–87)

1. Pope Benedict XVI, *Caritas in Veritate,* encyclical on integral human development, June 29, 2009, http://w2.vatican.va/content/benedict -xvi/en/encyclicals/documents/hf_ben-xvi_enc_20090629_caritas -in-veritate.html.

2. Michael Novak, "Pope Benedict XVI's *Caritas,*" *First Things* Web Exclusive, August 17, 2009, http://www.firstthings.com/web-exclusives /2009/08/pope-benedict-xvis-caritas/.

3. Novak, "The Pope, Liberty, and Capitalism," *National Review* 43, no. 11 (June 24, 1991): S-12.

4. George Weigel, "*Caritas in Veritate* in Gold and Red: The re- venge of Justice and Peace (or so they may think)," *National Re- view,* July 7, 2009, http://www.nationalreview.com/article/227839 /caritas-veritate-gold-and-red-george-weigel.

Chapter 8: Welfare to Be Dismantled? (pages 88–92)

1. Pope Francis, Address to the Participants in the Plenary of the Pon- tifical Council for Justice and Peace, October 2, 2014, https://w2.vatican .va/content/francesco/en/speeches/2014/october/documents/papa -francesco_20141002_pont-consiglio-giustizia-e-pace.html.

2. Mario Toso, "The Main Objectives of the Seminar and of the Working Paper," The Global Common Good: Towards a More Inclusive Economy, Vatican City, July 11–12, 2014, http://www.iustitiaetpax.va /content/dam/giustiziaepace/Eventi/globalcommongood/TOSO _EconomiaPovert%C3%A0_11luglio2014_ENG.pdf.

3. Qtd. in "La crisi? C'è anche perché la politica è succube della fi- nanza," *Vatican Insider, La Stampa,* July 7, 2014, http://vaticaninsider .lastampa.it/vaticano/dettaglio-articolo/articolo/toso-toso-toso-35208.

4. Qtd. in "Per Francesco i poveri sono la Chiesa, non un'appendice del Vangelo," *Vatican Insider, La Stampa,* August 5, 2014, http:// vaticaninsider.lastampa.it/inchieste-ed-interviste/dettaglio-articolo /articolo/francesco-francis-francisco-35608/.

Chapter 9: The Protection of Creation (pages 93–99)

1. Pope Francis, General Audience, June 5, 2013, http://w2.vatican .va/content/francesco/en/audiences/2013/documents/papa -francesco_20130605_udienza-generale.html.

2. Francis, Address to the Members of the Diplomatic Corps, January 13, 2014, http://w2.vatican.va/content/francesco/en/speeches/2014 /january/documents/papa-francesco_20140113_corpo-diplomatico.html.

3. Francis, Angelus, Febraury 9, 2014, http://w2.vatican.va /content/francesco/en/angelus/2014/documents/papa-francesco _angelus_20140209.html.

4. Francis, homily for the Solemnity of St. Joseph, March 19, 2013, http://w2.vatican.va/content/francesco/en/homilies/2013/documents /papa-francesco_20130319_omelia-inizio-pontificato.html.

5. Francis, General Audience, May 21, 2014, http://w2.vatican .va/content/francesco/en/audiences/2014/documents/papa -francesco_20140521_udienza-generale.html.

6. Francis, *Laudato Sì,* On Care for Our Common Home, encyclical, May 24, 2015, http://w2.vatican.va/content/francesco/en/encyclicals /documents/papa-francesco_20150524_enciclica-laudato-si.html.

Chapter 10: Land, Housing, and Work (pages 100–107)

1. Pope Francis, Address to the Participants in the World Meet- ing of Popular Movements, October 28, 2014, http://w2.vatican.va /content/francesco/en/speeches/2014/october/documents/papa -francesco_20141028_incontro-mondiale-movimenti-popolari.html.

Chapter 11: "Economic Systems That Must Make War in Order to Survive" (pages 108–15)

1. Francis, "Where is your brother?," morning meditation in the chapel of the *Domus Sanctae Marthae,* June 2, 2013, http://w2.vatican .va/content/francesco/en/cotidie/2013/documents/papa-francesco -cotidie_20130602_war-madness.html.

2. Francis, Angelus, September 8, 2013, http://w2.vatican.va/content /francesco/en/angelus/2013/documents/papa-francesco_angelus _20130908.html.

3. "Full text of Pope Francis' Interview with 'La Vanguardia,'" *Catholic News Agency,* June 13, 2014, http://www.catholicnewsagency.com /news/pope-francis-interview-with-la-vanguardia---full-text-45430/.

4. "The pope's divisions: Francis, capitalism and war," *Erasmus: Religion and public policy* blog, *The Economist,* June 20, 2014, http://www .economist.com/blogs/erasmus/2014/06/francis-capitalism-and-war.

5. In-Flight Press Conference from Korea to Rome, August 18, 2014, http://w2.vatican.va/content/francesco/en/speeches/2014/august /documents/papa-francesco_20140818_corea-conferenza-stampa.html.

6. Francis, homily on the Occasion of the 100th Anniversary of the Outbreak of the First World War, Redipuglia, Italy, September 13, 2014, http://w2.vatican.va/content/francesco/en/homilies/2014/documents /papa-francesco_20140913_omelia-sacrario-militare-redipuglia.html.

Chapter 12: Social Doctrine in a World Governed by Financial Technocrats (pages 116–30)

1. Ettore Gotti Tedeschi, *Amare Dio e fare soldi. Massime di economia divina,* Biblioteca Rosmini (Verona: Fede & Cultura, 2014).

Chapter 13: Capitalist Economy and Civil Market Economy (pages 131–38)

1. Stefano Zamagni, *Famiglia e lavoro: Opposizione o armonia?* (Milan: San Paolo Edizioni, 2012); *Impresa responsabile e mercato civile* (Bologna: Il Mulino, 2013).

2. Alan Greenspan, *The Map and the Territory: Risk, Human Nature, and the Future of Forecasting* (New York: Penguin, 2013).

Chapter 14: A Voice from the *Villas Miserias* (pages 139–46)

1. Silvina Premat, *Preti dalla fine del mondo: Viaggio tra i curas villeros di Bergoglio* (Bologna: EMI, 2014).

Epilogue: The Economy and the Gospel (pages 154–58)

1. Diego Alonso-Lasheras, "Evangelizzazione ed economia: denuncia e proposta," *Evangelii gaudium: il testo ci interroga* (Rome: Gregorian & Biblical Press, 2014), 224.

2. Ibid., 233.